Praise for
The Jeshua Collective

I am overwhelmed with tears of joy at the information that was given to me about my mother. I have found someone that I can trust with readings.

Jeshua Collective validated my mediumship abilities and walked me through what was happening with my own awakening. I was afraid of what was happening, I no longer feel paranoid. I am looking forward to the future instead of dread. It is heartwarming to know I have abilities. Thank you, Jeshua.

Jeshua is undeniably speaking through Carol. She (they) knew things about my life that is not on social media or available publicly. I am able to heal myself from my past and their guidance is undoubtedly the reason why.

I was hesitant to get a reading over the phone about my loved one, but within the first thirty seconds there was information that came through that was incredibly accurate (personality traits, physical issues, and words spoken before he passed). I am eternally grateful for finding Carol and her guides.

Carol, I feel so blessed to have found you. The channeled reading I had with you changed my life. You are the real deal.

Thank you, Carol, for a great healing of my dad's condition. He felt better immediately. I'm happy for the serendipity of life's unfoldment.

Books Written by Jeshua

<u>Channeled Works</u>

Ocularity of the Mind: Ocularity Series, Book 1 (2022)
Mind Body Connection: Mind Body Series, Book 1 (2022)

<u>Contribution</u>

Women Living In Alignment (2022)

At this publishing of this book there are fourteen additional works that have been channeled and are in queue for publishing, with more on the way. To stay in contact with us, please subscribe via the website: www.thepittsburghmedium.com

Mind Body CONNECTION

Create Your Reality
and Pave the Way to Your Intuitive Abilities

Mind Body Series
Book 1

CAROL COLLINS
Original Channel for The Jeshua Collective

Mind Body Connection
Create Your Reality and Pave the Way to Your Intuitive Abilities

Copyright © 2022

All rights reserved. No part of this book may be reproduced by any method for public or private use–other than for "fair use" as brief quotations embodied in articles and reviews–without prior written permission of the publisher.

The intent of the author is to provide general information to individuals who are taking positive steps in their lives for emotional and spiritual well-being. If you use any of the information in this book for yourself, the author and the publisher assume no responsibility for your actions. Readers are encouraged to seek the counsel of competent professionals with regards to such matters.

Powerful You! Publishing is committed to publishing works of quality and integrity. In that spirit, we are proud to offer this book to our readers; however, the story, the experiences, and the words are the author's alone.

Published by: Powerful You! Inc. USA
powerfulyoupublishing.com

LCCN: 2022920340

Carol Collins – First Edition

ISBN: 978-1-959348-03-0

First Edition November 2022

BODY MIND & SPIRIT / Channeling & Mediumship

Dedication

To the one who brought me into, and will bring me out of, this physical life for a purpose that was beyond my comprehension and beyond my own abilities as a human being. You are my favorite, always! For loving me as much as you, evidently have, lifetime after lifetime. James Edward Murray – WE DID IT! ♥

To all of the inaugural I AM Intensive (June 2021) weekend participants without whom I would not have accomplished what my Higher Self was hoping to. Your energy, your belief in Jeshua, and the entire Collective of Beings that comprise them, added to my own restart button. I treasure you. You heard it first – "Don't not do it" and "Be fancy." Happy manifesting! Much love to you all.

Table of Contents

Books Written by Jeshua	ii
Dedication	v
A Pillar 2 Book	viii
The Essential Material - The 4 Pillars of Learning	ix
Note From Author	x
The Introduction	xi
Chapter 1 ~ Reclaim Joy	1
Chapter 2 ~ Thoughts Create Things	27
Chapter 3 ~ Telepathy Renewed	47
Chapter 4 ~ Taking of the Baton	67
Chapter 5 ~ Refinement	83
Chapter 6 ~ Multiplier Effect	91
Chapter 7 ~ Partner Up	101
Chapter 8 ~ Unravelling	113
Chapter 9 ~ Inter-Mind Communication	123
Chapter 10 ~ Retraining Is Necessary	137
Chapter 11 ~ Manifesting On Purpose	151
Chapter 12 ~ The Number Sequence	165
Chapter 13 ~ Your Identity	179
Chapter 14 ~ Aura-Seekers	187
Opportunities to Engage with Jeshua	193
About the Author	197

A Pillar 2 Book

The following dictation was received in channeled state in July and November 2021. It was captured in 17 video recorded sessions over a span of 6 days and totaling 10.5 hours.

The Essential Material

The Four Pillars of Learning

PILLAR 1: The Foundational Material - The starting point for understanding who «Source Beings» are, who we are, and why we are having this life experience.

PILLAR 2: Idea Reconstruction - Otherwise known as law of attraction, deliberate creation; verbal therapy; and using the power of thought energy to manifest your life, on purpose.

PILLAR 3: Directed Energy for Self-Healing - Moving Source Frequency within "the grid" as a means of clearing unconscious beliefs that stop and/or delay your ability to connect with your Guide team and manifest a life of abundance.

PILLAR 4: Intuitive Development - Verbal and vibrational instruction to open your inter-mind to ocular (mind's eye) to increase your ability to receive, clarity in that receiving, and accuracy on what your Guide is conveying to you.

Note From Author

Be at peace as you read this. Breathe softly, exhale fully. For within these pages are weavings of intellect, of Source frequency as well as Knowledge. The team of Beings that I call my nonphysical best friends are Teachers, let the capitalization of that word be meaningful to you. It is by their doing that it is written that way. They are here to guide us, to teach us, to clean out our clogged pipes—so that we all "get stuff" on purpose. I love that! I love this topic and most of all I love that you have chosen it. They are with you as you read it, guiding you back to it and to certain pages that are meaningful for you at the moment you read it. Occasionally, let the book fall open and read just the page or paragraph that you are drawn to. Write down what you understood. Then, later on continue reading as usual. Your abilities will rise each time you do.

Love, Carol

The Introduction

Session: 1, video: #0016
April 24, 2021

To Our Dear Readers

    Ocularity of the mind is something that we want all of you to have. You were meant to have it and you do not. Those of you that do have it, good. Those of you that do not, learn it. How do you learn it? From us, not a human being, preferably. Human beings teach you what they think they know, and their teaching is incomplete at best.
    Teachers teach you what they have learned. They teach you what they have been taught. But what they have been taught is wrong because you do not ask enough questions. I want you to ask more questions. I want you to have more interesting questions because I want you to be creative. How do you be creative if you are not? Slow your thinking down. Be someone who doodles, and while you are doodling make a note of any sensations that you have in your body. Then ask why. For example, "Why did that happen? Why am I doodling?" Then expand to anything, such as, "Where did the word doodle come from?"
    I want you to be creative in your questions and I want you to feel for the answers. When you do, I know if it is your mind putting itself front and center and answering the question, or if it was a received thought from us. A human

teacher has no idea. They have some games for you to play, and most of them are good. But they cannot validate for you whether you received or imagined something. They have some generalizations that are also wrong because they do not know what your mind is ready for. They just know what they have been taught.

For example, a "human straightforward" teacher might say, "If you see something crystal-clear, it is received. If you can see it twice in a row and it looks identical, it is received." Well, that is categorically wrong. The mind can produce the same image again and again. Look about your world, look about your room. The mind sees things, it remembers them, it produces them.

We are not robots; we are intelligence in the ethers. Through the ethers we create and we communicate and we partner with you. This thing called life in the physical reality is meant for creativity. It is meant for learning. It is meant for doing. It is meant for being. It is meant for having—with us. Only, this world has evolved itself to have forgotten how to communicate with us. So here we are, teaching you how to do it.

We are going to have a good time in this book, so sit back and relax. There will be some things that you are not ready to hear and that is okay. If you get irritated reading the book, stay with it because it is meant to shake you up some. It is meant to tell your mind that it has learned incorrectly from human beings.

We want the mind to hear those words because we want the mind, the inner-mind, to pay attention to us and not rely on what you see and what you hear as gospel. We want the

The Introduction

mind to get curious and to seek us out and seek our Knowing on that same subject. We want the mind to slow down in its response time, and it will. You will know that it is doing something different because your emotions will get a little wobbly for a while. They will settle down and then life will be new and different in a positive way.

Mind Body Connection. Let us begin.

CHAPTER 1

Reclaim Joy

*The tone of us is purity.
You have learned that God is purity.
It leverages this understanding
and resolves the differences in its learning.
It registers that we are—meaning we feel—like purity.
There is no roughness in our vibrational tone.*

Chapter 1 ~ Reclaim Joy

Session: 2
Channeled July 16, 2021

Once in a while, we have a person who allows us to speak through them, and that is Carol in this moment. There are others, of course, but we speak through her now. Who are we? Jeshua. We are a collective of nonphysical Beings who have mastered all things. We know we sound boastful. It truly is just a statement of fact.

Carol has invited us into her life in a way that is meaningful to us. She wanted us to say "meaningful to her," but we said meaningful to us because to do book-writing we need a person who is willing to set aside a Friday evening, as she is tonight. Carol sits here and lets us speak through her. There is no one else home; there is no one else truly in her life right now that is willing to sit with her and videotape the asking of questions, allowing us to teach.

It is what she loves most. She has students who are interested and eager to learn, but they have lives. She has us. We say this because we want you to know what she does. She does still work during the day, although she does not want to. She wants to do this all day—readings, attunements, book-writing, answering questions, classes, workshops—but she wants people to be there and right now she is new to the channeling world. We love her, but love only gets you just so far because the human being has a mind that plays a part.

(At the publication of this book this, finally, is no longer true. This is Jeshua to speak. Carol followed guidance, followed structured guidance to get where she—and we—wanted her to be, working and doing this book and others

like it. To give readings daily and plan vacation-like seminars and do it during the day without competition of time, of employer, of responsibility, of desire. She is at work with us fully.)

We have to abide by the laws of this world and the laws include a belief that God is not real. We say "God" because that is the belief marker. But, truly, it means the attractor within, the sub-conscious mind, that does not think. It lives after your body fades away. It thinks one and done.

It hears stories about "God"; it does not believe them. Why? Because the stories are inconsistent. They say God loves, but that God destroys. The attractor within knows that we are present in your life. It does hear us—that is intuition. That is the quiet, silent, indirect guidance that you call a "gut feeling." It knows us and it knows our vibrational tone as purity and love.

It hears stories about "God"—God loves, God destroys, God loves, God kills, God loves, God maims, God loves some. But even after you perish God judges you, which means God does not love you. The inner-mind has decided in this world that the stories are stories. It does not believe that God is real.

It does not know the vibrational tone that it feels giving it gentle guidance. It does not have a name for us, for it just knows us as a pure, consistent, unwavering sound. It knows us as sound, and it loves us. No matter what religion, no matter what continent, no matter what the origin is, no matter who the iconic person is, there are stories of love and stories of judgment. Unceasing, unrelenting, unforgiving judgment.

Some of you are going to say, "Well, that is not true,

Chapter 1 ~ Reclaim Joy

there are so many peaceful religions." We say no, there are religions where the doctrine is softer but there are still rules. The rules are: Do not do this; do this or else. Do not do this; do this or else.

We do not have an "or else." We prefer that you do this, but if you do that, okay. We will guide you to what we want you to do and we will never stop leading you to it. As long as you are focused in this physical life, we have our eyes on you the entire time. We never leave your side, we never blink.

Those that might have an opportunity to watch the video of this dictation will witness Carol, this woman, having a moment where her mind is registering the fact we just spoke about—it is causing her body to heat up. It is registering within itself that the voice that is speaking through her is what the stories mean as God. The tone of us is purity. You have learned that God is purity. It leverages this understanding and resolves the differences in its learning. It registers that we are—meaning we feel—like purity. There is no roughness in our vibrational tone. Zero.

The mind of the channel cannot not open up to disbelieving the beliefs that are resident in this world. It feels the tone of us and hears the words we speak. We refer again and again to "us" and that we are speaking through the human being. It learns that it is not producing the words and that we are. Slowly but surely, the mind of the human being that we speak through learns that we are Real.

In every single human being, when the mind releases something that it held onto that was not good for it, the human body cries. Very briefly, then, it feels the presence of us swoop in and the tears stop. How long does it take to reclaim joy? Seventeen seconds or less. It cannot be longer, not in this world, not ever. If there are tears that last longer then it is not a moment of releasing, a moment of self-forgiveness for not understanding that the stories bore truth yet were laced with words derived by men to maintain the balance of power.

There is in this world something called energy. There is the kind that you call electricity and you turn the lights on, you start your appliances. The kind where you blow dry your hair, open your tin cans, leaf-blowers, lawnmowers, televisions, clock radios. Darn near everything uses electricity. Car batteries, for some.

We are not electric Beings; we are electromagnetic intelligence, and we created the worlds that you are in, so we know a thing or two about them. We are not dead people, although we are. Our bodies have faded away, but the Soul of each person we have been simply steps into the nonphysical dimension and continues along its upward ascension. It continues as the person with the same name that it had been given at birth, forevermore.

What does that Being do after Transition? Anything it wants. It learns, it grows, it does things over again, it visits people, it receives guidance, it tries things, it passes information on. Any number of things.

In the very beginning, when Carol began to receive us in this way, she was speaking to her Loved One in spirit that initially gave the name James Edward Murray—very deliberately, spelled out with the nose. That Being played a part in a past life and knows her, albeit by a different name. They had a life together where they loved each other.

Chapter 1 ~ Reclaim Joy

Prior to coming into this life as Carol, that Being knew what her Intentions were, and said, "I will be there for you. I love you. It matters not if your Soul Essence is in another human form; male or female, it matters not. I know you as a glorious nonphysical vibrational Being and I love you. I also knew you as a human being and since you are going to do something that has to do with that life, I will be there as I have every time that you have used that past life to do something." And so it is.

It was that Being that was the first to be present with her as we began direct communication, direct contact, first contact, Day 1. There were other "day ones" that Carol knows about now, but that was the very first day there was undeniable conversation from a nonphysical Being who wanted to speak with her. He did not answer questions using an image or two or three, or a phrase that she could piece together, understanding. It was a "Let us sit down and have a conversation, you and I." It was two-way dialogue from the beginning. "I am James, and I am glad to meet you again."

Each time she has come into this life to undo something that that Being knows about, they meet, she finds him in spirit, and they begin again. It is the way that her Higher Self has decided to work through suicide. When someone takes their own life, does something to the human form that they cannot come back from, they must remove the memory of it from their Being. Not the memory of it happening, but the desire for it to have had a moment point.

When a human being has a strong desire, or is at a crossroads—and both are meaningful—there are two pathways. In the moment just prior to taking one's life, there is always doubt and there is always a second pathway. That second pathway must be discovered by that person in another lifetime.

There are many things that can be done in the nonphysical in order for the human being to be able to go where they need to in their mind to be able to, not undo, exactly, but choose differently. For Carol, it was France. She knows the town now. She knows the name and that there are still living relatives in that town, as well as in the United States. She has spoken to one. She desires to go to France; we say, not yet. Soon we will take her where she has asked to go and, if she is brave enough, she will knock on the door of one of those relatives.

We say not yet because we want her to have a little more recognition in the world so that she is welcomed for who she is now. She also does not speak French so there will be a need for an interpreter. That is the easy part. It has been not a long road, but it has been several lifetimes where it has been desired to undo some of the pattern that caused that human being to take its own life.

If you are here in the physical body and you are experiencing something in life, say indigestion, and you narrow the cause down to the types of food you eat, you can begin to choose different foods. Not only choose differently while being somewhat angry at having to do so, but also find your way to choosing happily, by free will choice that does not upset your physical body. You may not have chosen indigestion, but you chose food and that food did not agree with you and therefore you received indigestion. By re-choosing happily, you have undone the desire for your

Chapter 1 ~ Reclaim Joy

previous choice.

The same thing with heartache. You have a heartache over a love gone wrong. If that heartache is addressed here in the physical world, and you learn to not be sad or depressed or angry or hateful or ambivalent, and instead you learn simply to pick yourself up and keep going with life and look forward to the next falling in love activity, be it with life or a person, then you have undone that previous experience.

For those that have decided to take their life, they lost the opportunity to make different choices. We are not angry ever, not even then. It simply alters what it is that the larger part of them, the entity, the broader part of their spirit Being, can do in successive lifetimes. They now add to the plan, and they must keep adding to the plan until the circumstances that caused the desire and the action to remove themselves from this world is addressed completely.

What does that look like? I give you an example. Someone is heartbroken and they decided to end their life. There were things that led up to feeling heartbroken—shame, remorse, guilt, anger, abandonment issues, inferiority complexes, doubt of all kinds. In future lives of that person, they must address one by one the emotions that caused them to be afraid of life. Sooner or later, all of those elements will be addressed.

The how and when and the who are not always known because free will is a component of this world. You cannot get away from that, even if you try. Human beings in the world today, quite frankly, do not have enough channeled readings! If you had them with us, The Jeshua Collective, we would sit you down and say, "Dear one, we love you so much. This is where you have got it all wrong, but this is where you are on the path." We would map out your life's Intentions for you and show you why you have this pattern, why you have that pattern—similar or dissimilar to another person in your family or anybody else.

All these comparisons that you do are unnecessary. We talk to you about why you are the middle child, the eldest child, the only child, the only survivor as a twin because there is always meaning behind your start. That is all. Your Soul Being does not set you up to experience heartbreak so that you can release the memory of it. No. Anyone that disagrees with us is wrong one hundred percent of the time.

Each Soul Being decides what it wants to do in a lifetime, and then chooses the perfect components to aid in that desire. It angles itself through the dimensions and is deposited into the world. When you do this, you are enveloped by an etheric field. That etheric field contains your Guides. We are all in this together, and that is truth.

Your Guide helps you in and draws you out. That Being does not reside within the body with you, but never leaves your side. They come into this world with you and participates in your entire life. They persuade you gently, nudging quietly—*Go this way, go that way. Do this, not that. Talk to this one, not that one. Put that down, pick this up. Look around the corner. Perfect. Good job.*

You have blinders on in this life. We all know you do. We know you cannot hear us. We love you so much because you cannot. You are doing this thing called being a human being, and you knew that you would not be able to hear us. You hoped that your person, whoever you grew up to be,

Chapter 1 ~ Reclaim Joy

would find the desire for communication with us. But if they did not, it would be okay. You had things that you wanted to get done, and if you found your way to them, they would feel delightful. They would feel like powerful knowing. It would register as a "I have to do this—you couldn't tear me away from it if you tried" kind of thing. On occasion, you do find the desire to communicate with us.

We love every single one of you, and we love you even when you get it wrong.

We train the mind to hear us, and when you find your way to us we begin the Unfoldment (capital U). The Unfoldment is not what people think it is. The Unfoldment is a Plan and it is designed by your Guides. The Higher Self decides the Intentions and it also plays a part in the Unfoldment, but the Unfoldment Plan is designed by the Guides. Why? Because the Guides are at a level higher and know more about how to bring about the abilities (your abilities) that are wanted by the Higher Self.

The Unfoldment goes like this: Highest Guide, Ascended Guide, Jeshua the entity, and the Higher Self of the human being. If the Highest Guide is not at the master level, there is also a Master brought in among them. We then have a conversation that goes something like this: "Higher Self, your person is doing well. They're starting to have an interest in knowing how to communicate with us. Do you want to proceed down the path of the desire of the human being?" Higher Self says yay, or, "No, I think that if I allow my person to go the route they are interested in it will stop us from being able to discover something on our path later in life." We look at it, and we are always in agreement because the Higher Self knows their person completely.

There are other, similar situations in which the Higher Self would say no. What kind of things? Satanic worship, cults, and things of that nature, because they are obstacles to knowing who we are. They increase the separation; they do not resolve it. It is allowed at times because sometimes being further away (increasing the separation) does not harm the Intentions (capital I). Although, human beings, you get to decide, and if you walk into a situation that you know is not good you get to experience what it feels like to have known that that experience was not good for you. That is called remorse.

We never allow without doing something about it. Those feelings of strange discernment—you might say foreboding, you might say fear, you might say worried, you might say scared, you might say obstinate—those are all indicators that your Guides are surrounding you, asking you to turn away. *Turn away, you do not want to do this. Turn away, turn away, turn away. You do not want to do this.*

Why do we not just halt you? Because you are allowed to decide the direction of your life. You are not puppets on a string, none of you. Even those of you that have predetermined decisions.

Carol, for instance; it was known that she would channel and, if she did, we knew that she would want to write books. It was built-in to do that activity. She has always been a book reader. She has had this desire to be an author. She never followed through on it but that is why the desire was there. "I just want to write a book, maybe a poetry book, maybe a leadership book, maybe some affirmation cards, maybe a

Chapter 1 ~ Reclaim Joy

self-help book, maybe a book about me. I think I'm going to write a book about my life. As a matter of fact, I'm going to start and I think the chapters are going to look like this..." She has all of those notes still at the writing of this book. She has not followed through on those things on her own, although we have written a number of books through her.

If it is not built-in—and most things are not—you get to choose. If you choose to do something that causes you worry or worse, that is us asking you to step away. Step away for now or forever, depending on the situation. But is always us because the mind is focused on something unhealthy and when it is, we come in and we give a different opinion. *Do this, you'll enjoy it better, do this you'll enjoy it better, do this you'll enjoy it better.*

The mind registers one thing, a different opinion. When a different opinion is present it does not know where it is coming from and it creates a vibration within the body. It is listening. The listening is the vibration of guidance. You have created negative emotions because of it. It is, and has always been, guidance to move you away from point A, toward point B. Now the mind thinks that there is something wrong with the body because of it and causes you to feel afraid, or sad, or lonely, or depressed, et cetera.

The mind simply misunderstands what the inner-mind is doing. The inner-mind is listening, although the inner-mind does not know how to translate what we are saying. That is the whole point of this book. The inner-mind listens for us, it wants to talk to us, but it has no idea what we are saying because we speak a vibration. It is what we speak—a vibration that needs to be translated by your human mind.

We teach you how in meditation.

There is intelligence embedded within the vibration, as well as—in later stages—instructions for the mind. The mind does not know how to translate until we teach it, and we cannot teach it until you sit and rest your mind. Not sleep, but resting your mind from all of the thoughts that are racing through it. Then we get to work.

What are we working on? The Unfoldment, your life's Plan specific to communication with us. There are other aspects of your Unfoldment Plan. The conversation takes everything into account. Those that have been identified as your Teachers in the nonphysical—you, the human being, your nonphysical Teachers—they come together and decide your Unfoldment, the Plan for what your abilities will be.

Will everybody become a channel? No. Do we want everybody to be a channel? Yes. Why do we not just decide the Unfoldment for everyone to be a channel? Because sometimes your bodies do not agree with that type of training. The mind is too quick or too slow or too fixated on something. Sometimes the human being (we foresee it ahead of time) will not have an interest in anything except tarot. Tarot will capture their attention; they will fall in love with it, and there they will stay. We never make a Plan that will be displeasing to the human being.

Can we adjust the Plan? No, because we never get it wrong. Once the Unfoldment is designed, we begin asking your mind to practice listening to us, understanding who we are, knowing what each element of the vibration means. It is a language. We are teaching the mind a language! We are teaching the mind, the inner-mind, a language.

Chapter 1 ~ Reclaim Joy

Unfoldment into mediumship classes through the Spiritualist church or any other that says, "Sit down and let me teach you how to increase your intuition. I, the human being straightforward, will teach you how to connect to Spirit," is wrong! You can teach a human being how to follow your instructions, but you do not know how to teach the inner-mind how to translate vibrational technology any more than you can take the output, the vibrational output, of a computer and understand it. You need the guts of the computer and the application and the programs to be able to spell it out for you in your language.

The mind can learn and we know all languages and we focus on your mind and give it exactly what it is ready for. The human being might want to be on a platform in a month. The inner-mind might be terrified of being in front of people. When it is positioned on the platform with the human being as its host, it shuts down and the human being fails to receive. Then the human being receives shame or embarrassment, or both.

We tell students when they are ready to practice outside of class. We tell students when they are ready to receive on a platform in front of an audience. We tell students when they are ready to receive payment and on what kind of questions and in what type of environment and for how long. How about that for guidance?

We have students who received well when they are not under pressure. Twenty minutes is a good receiving—taking it slow, following their Guides, looking for the partnering that has been identified for them. It may be to know when a new subject is coming, when the current subject is complete, or where we are going with the conversation, meaning the way we are explaining what we want the person to know.

But add pressure like money or a family member or being in front of strangers or a question that is also on the mind of the reader, and stress rears up and blocks the path of receiving. The human being who was otherwise ready for casual back and forth exchange now has an inner-mind that has shut down. The receiving will not occur or will be incorrect or unclean.

Unclean simply means contaminated—and we mean contaminated! It could also simply be inaccurate. The mind can contaminate a small amount and add a word here or there and give a little extra, or it can contaminate by a lot and change the entire meaning. The human being can do the same thing when describing an image, adding an assumption to a word or phrase. We say do not do it. Always validate early, and often, for yourself. When you do, you slow down, and when you slow down you are more accurate.

We train the mind in every case. When you go to class with a human being straightforward and they are talking about pendulums, for instance, they are giving a lesson. At the same time, if your mind is quiet, we are giving our own lesson to your mind. We play along if the teacher has an exercise and supplement theirs with ours. We do not stop what we have planned for you, but we help you to participate in class because it is a desire of yours; otherwise, you would not be there. Even if you are feeling strange about a certain exercise, we know that you want to participate and so we help you. If your mind is not quiet then we participate with you by teaching your mind to hear us and allow us to help

Chapter 1 ~ Reclaim Joy

you with the exercise at hand.

We want you to go to development circles and we want you to practice without pressure. We want you to play in those development circles. We do not want you to practice giving meaningful readings. We want you to do circles with a channel or with a very strong clairvoyant/medium who is willing to put their own ego aside and ask their Guides to guide them as the teacher.

We are knowing what your minds need. When it comes to learning how to communicate with us, we not only are the Teachers of how to do it, we are the instructors for the inner-mind on how to learn another language—OURS!

There is so much to do in this life. We want you to have fun and we want you to have fun developing your abilities to communicate with us. Is it not fun to be right? Is it not fun to be validated? It is fun for us, Source Beings, your Loved Ones, Spirit Helpers, to say, "Well done, good job, nice received thought! Excellent description of what was sent. Best effort ever. Let's try again." Then we continue.

Do we encourage? Yes. Do human beings, in their teacher role, encourage? Sometimes. Do we know what is going on in the inner-mind? Always. We are watching it extremely carefully—whenever we are teaching the mind who we are, what we are doing, and that we want it to pay attention to us for communication. We look for all indicators that the mind is uneasy. It is our Knowing when it is coming and we stop before the mind gets there.

We do know all things and we are not linear. Can human beings in their teacher role do that? No, they cannot. Not one. We do not mind when teachers, in their desire to convey to people how to do what they do, communicate with us (assuming they do it) and come up with a curriculum; we love it. Not every person in the class is ready for pendulums or whatever the lesson of the night is. That is why we want teachers to tune into their Guides during class—not to give readings, but to give specialized attention or instructions to this one or that one or the entire class. We know who is there and we know what their Unfoldment is. The teacher does not—a human teacher, that is.

We follow the inner-mind when we teach. If it wants, we give. If it wants a lot, we give some and then we make a decision what comes next. We not only teach the mind who we are and how to communicate with us, we remind the mind that we are Source. We will never encourage the mind to believe that it (the inner-mind) is us. The mind can simulate, the mind can add extra, and the mind can pretend to be us. If it does, it means that it has closed the door on us. Then the human being receives telepathic or simulated conversation. People wonder why their readings are inaccurate and this is the reason. Telepathy or "going psychic" can create an opportunity for some details to be validated, but it is not a skill that is useful. It is registering thoughts of another person, not guidance from the Spirit Beings who are providing Knowledge (capital K).

We are Teachers on how to stop the mind from going psychic, from attempting to use telepathy rather than turning to us for guidance. We are the Teachers in all cases, even when the human being, the student, has no idea that we are. We do not mind that you do not know this because we know you have blinders on. We explain that we are the Teachers

Chapter 1 ~ Reclaim Joy

so that more of you understand what the Unfoldment is and who is doing it. We are. For you, not to you.

We are providing our Knowing about communicating with Source, and our knowledge is vast. We teach the mind on cue every time your mind is quiet. Little by little—eventually, a lot by a lot—your mind understands. When you love it, you get more. When you are nervous about it, you stand still. When you get excited, you get more. When you get super-excited, you stand still. When you enjoy it, you get a lot more.

We want you to get a lot more and be accurate.

Learning how to channel comes about from you and your Highest Level having a conversation again and again and again. There is nothing that we will not teach your mind. Creativity is desired. You want to sit and give readings? Excellent. What do you want to know? What do you want to be good at? What do you want to be known for? What is your desired specialty?

We will teach you how to see visions, make them move, make them colorful, make them unfold into a scene, show you faces up close, far away, or give you details. We will train your mind for a Symbol or two or ten or show you how to physically identify who is present in the conversation. We will hand-select past lives and Loved Ones to aid you in life on a certain subject, or two or ten. Teach you to increase complexity so you see an image and a received knowing simultaneously of what the image is or who it is about. We will teach you different ways of identifying subjects by isolating the question, by locating and deciphering which Being is speaking and to whom, because sometimes—a little unknown fact—we are speaking to the reader and giving them some information that will aid them in their description of what comes next. A scarce few have understood that at times there is a moment of conversation that is private for them so that they can convey information easier.

We like to use physical sensations to convey meaning. Carol has an indicator in the bridge of her nose so that when she is giving a reading and feels it, she pauses for a moment and looks up and to the right in the way she does, and knows that we have something to say to her. Readers are not always validated, and this is a way of helping them. Sometimes the human being that is receiving a reading is very uptight, focused on the question, focused on the situation, focused on the time and how much time has gone by, and whether they will be able to ask all of their questions. Whether they are enjoying the reading or not, there is stress involved. When there is, it is more difficult to hear the answer. We can help the reader to know when this is the case. It is fun to partner with us.

Channeled readings are always verbal. We say what we want to say, how we want to say it, for as long as the channel allows us to speak. A human being can clamp down; they can constrict their muscles and hold back. When this occurs we pause and wait, and when they have brought themselves back into center, we continue. We see it coming, and we pause. We are all-knowing, all-powerful, all-intelligent, all-encompassing, all-eyes-focused-on-you type of Beings—as are you after you make your Transition.

There is time to learn; no studying is involved. There are things that human beings want to know, such as the

Chapter 1 ~ Reclaim Joy

current lingo, so they can feel knowledgeable when they go to a class or a seminar or a workshop or watch a video. Everyone wants to feel included and sometimes that does mean understanding terminology, so we talk about that now.

Empath first, clairaudient next, then clairvoyant. We stop there for this one reason: those are the areas that we speak to. We speak to the body, we speak to the ear, we speak to the mind. No others.

We know there is a list of "clairs" out there and we have even added to it, but there are only three places that can receive and interpret a vibrational Knowing: the body and its energy receptors placed around your physical form; the inner ear; and your brain. There are receptors in each of those three places and those three places have embedded within them the ability to not only receive but to translate and transmit Knowledge from us.

The ability of an empath—in this world, in this day and time—is an ability that is all but lost. The body receives communication and is unsure what to do with it. It creates a vibration and, as we have said, the mind misunderstands why the vibration is being put into action and it creates an emotion instead. The intelligent receptors that have the ability to translate vibrational communication are now dumb. Their ability to receive and understand instructions, to be able to learn how to translate, have been watered down –if that feels better to you. The ability to easily translate vibrational tones is no longer fully intact, and therefore extremely difficult. It is not that you cannot do it, but that it is not strong in the world anymore. The human beings that are here now have preferred verbal communication over physical communication and the physical body has adapted to that preference. That is all.

When we say translate, we mean translate just like your ear does—the human physical body. Does that mean that your belly button could understand Knowledge of the Universe? Yes. Well, it is not your belly button, but there are receptor points all over the body. Those receptor points simply light up and they begin to vibrate. They no longer have the ability to translate; they vibrate only. When they vibrate, the mind associates an emotion. Depending on how many of those receptors have been turned on at any one time, the mind distinguishes some versus more, versus a lot.

When some are turned on you feel happy or unhappy, depending on the circumstances. When more are turned on, depending on where it falls in the quantity spectrum, it equals very happy or very unhappy. If a lot are turned on, then not only are you happy but you understand us clearly. As we have said, what we have said here, the human physical form no longer has many receptors turned on at the same time. It is why we are writing this book and why we re-train the mind in meditation.

Now, the ear. We can also send Knowledge to the ear. The ear (when audient ability is present) does not produce the likeness of hearing when we do, it simply translates. It is a translation mechanism that occurs—in the body, in the ear, or the mind. True audient people are people whose ear still has the ability to translate communication that is coming from the nonphysical dimension. Very rare, but there are still some.

Does that mean that you hear voices in the room if you

Chapter 1 ~ Reclaim Joy

have the audient ability? No. It means that you might see pictures in your mind. It is translating Knowledge, translating instructions, and transferring it to your mind. It has nothing to do with hearing. We know the entire world's population is going to argue with Carol and she is going to say, "I didn't say it, but I do understand it."

We want you all to understand this clearly. It is three and one. You know the concept. You have three areas, three types of areas, which can receive and interpret and translate and then transmit to the mind conversation that comes from your Guides. There are receptors in the body, there are receptors in the inner ear, and there are receptors within the brain, and then all transmit that knowing to your mind as conversation from us.

Your brain is the one that all of you can use. It is the most mature. When the brain receives, interprets, translates, and transmits, it sends what it has received to a different part of the brain to produce the likeness of whatever we said or asked of it.

We simply say ocular, audient, empath (or physical), audient, mind's eye. Take your pick. There are three and only three, and we are the ones that train the physical body to do whatever it is that has been determined by the Higher Self (Unfoldment Plan). If the Higher Self says, "Audient, please, that is what I want to bring out in this one," then we do it. We do not neglect the other two, but we do them in accordance with the Plan.

Now, all these clairs that are in the world—what are they? They simply go like this: mind's eye seeing internal; mind's eye seeing external; mind's eye smelling; mind's eye tasting; mind's eye feeling; mind's eye hearing the likeness of myself; mind's eye hearing the likeness of others; mind's eye knowing, and then knowing very quickly. So quickly, indeed, that you say it as fast as you receive it—that's channeling.

Then there is a mind that is so delighted, so much in love with us that it looks to us for communication. But the human being has beliefs about God or possession or other things that cause them not to be able to move fully into a state of mind that is necessary for us to borrow the voice. They are not channeling, but their mind is supple. In that way, we can bring the mind interior to itself, load it up with information, and then bring the mind back to the surface. We then simply press a button and the human being starts to repeat everything that we just deposited in it. We call that a "resident channel," or someone who is "a channel."

Then there is a human being who has a soft and supple mind and who has also released limiting beliefs about who we are and no longer believes that there is an opposite of Love, that there are bad Spirits, negative Energies, evil Beings to be afraid of. That human being can partner with us and we teach the mind to move into an altered state. We sometimes describe it as a "different position within the mind" or a "room inside itself." We sit next to it and we ask the mind to say this and this and this and this and this and this and this (and we show you this image) and then say this and this and this and this…for as long as the mind will sit still in that place. That is a trance channel. A trance channel may be consciously aware or unconsciously aware—it depends on which beliefs have been unblocked and removed.

Chapter 1 ~ Reclaim Joy

We want all of you to be consciously aware, trance channels. Why? Because it means that you have removed blocks that were on your pathway in life. It means that you have decreased or removed beliefs about Source Beings being angry or judgmental or not Real. It means that you have discarded the notion of possession as foolishness, and rightly so. At this stage we can borrow the voice and say what we want to say, the way we want to say it.

A trance channel means that your mind is in the best position to learn, that your fears about who we are have diminished to the point where they are gone or so minuscule that they do not play a part. This allows us to convey meaning in the way that we intend it and not be subjected to human beings attempting to convey meaning for us.

We know how much people love to talk; so do we. We do prefer to say it ourselves, because then we convey the meaning that we are wanting to convey. We give the instructions that we are wanting to offer, and we do not add assumptions. We do not add opinions. We give Knowledge from the Universe that is Truth (capital T).

We guide you and we love you and we play with you. We want you to be friendly with us. We want people to use games to advance your learning to take the pressure off of being right, to take the pressure off from giving a reading and having to be right. Games and play should be forefront in every student's training curriculum. It allows the human being to practice without pressure.

End chapter.

CHAPTER 2

Thoughts Create Things

In each segment of your day there is this ongoing dance of I think, I do, I attract, we pull back. I think, I do, I attract, we pull back. I think, I do, I attract, we amplify because we do that as well. We are the backup system to your law of attraction.

Chapter 2 ~ Thoughts Create Things

Session: 3, video: #0018
July 17, 2021

Personal conveyance to Carol: Okay, now we are going to write this book but we are going to write the session details down on paper first. Number one, this is another chapter to the book Mind Body Connection and is Chapter Two. Recording is going, we're sitting in the chair. We have no cat, but the cat will come.

NOTE: I gave this to Carol at the beginning of our session because her mind was aware of the need for details and did not know how to produce them. Her mind was aware but not willing to go into a level deeper than her usual light state (of trance). Offering her mind these details put it at ease. Sometimes it takes a bit longer and sometimes none are needed. Personal guidance comes in many forms. This guidance was for the inner-mind and not her consciously-aware self. Although, she did appreciate my saying the date, chapter, and number so she could easily annotate it in her archive.

I am a Being within The Jeshua Collective and I am teaching through this woman. The teaching that I am giving has to do with the mind and the body in the human physical world. The human physical world is where you are. We are not where you are because we are not in that dimension. We are Beings who are able to view your dimension with extreme precision. That is how your Loved Ones know where you are. That is how your Guides know where you are. That is how I know that Carol is ready to have me speak through her. Why? Because I am watching her.

I am viewing your world. Can I see all of it at the same time? If I wanted to. Can I zero in and look at a fly's wings or hair on top of your head? I do not do that, but I could. Why do I not? Because it is not what I do. If I were someone who decided to be a caretaker of flora and fauna, then I would if there was a need for it. I just use it as an example.

I pause here and explain why because there will be a need for it. Someone will have the question about why not. *Do you not care about the little things? Is it that you only care about the people that you are speaking through? Do you only care about the ones that you knew?* No. We care about every single person. There is a part of me that is participating broadly in the world. There is a part of me that is participating with Entities that are guiding you. There are those that I am still providing direction for—not as the Highest Level, but as the Ascended One and, believe it or not, all of you will, at some point in your existence, reach the level that I have.

I have not always been at this level, but I have been here for quite some time, and it is a newer experience for me. In human years, I have been here maybe a hundred years—that is "new." What do I do here? I teach and I heal. I help heal the world, and I teach those of you in the nonphysical that are still learning how to do different things in the world.

What is my specialty? Travel. How to travel, when to travel, where to go, how to do it, what kind of things can you do, how to perceive experiences while you are there, how to perceive it before you get there, how to do it on your own, how to do it with someone, how to teach people how to do it. I say "people," and I do mean nonphysical Beings.

Chapter 2 ~ Thoughts Create Things

But I also teach human people because human beings are interested in how to do what you call projection. You will never get it right because your minds are not capable of it. Is that a limitation? No, because this linear world that you live in is not real. So it is not a limitation, it just happens to be a circumstance. How do you like that? It is a circumstance.

I have my eyes on this woman, Carol, daily. She has a Highest-Level Guide that is not me that watches her unceasingly. They live this life with her and everybody has that. I go into this a little bit here. You are not alone in this world, even when you choose to be physically, because your Guides cannot leave your side, nor would they. It is an impossibility.

If you do not hear us or see us or talk to us then you might feel as though you are alone, and I understand that perfectly well. I have had a number of lifetimes where I too felt abandoned. I do recall the feeling. I do not close in on it and retrace my steps because I find that to be a futile, useless thing to do.

If I were planning a lifetime where I wanted to use the memory of such an experience, where abandonment was plentiful, I still would not dive into the emotional content of a past experience of it. What would I do? Know it existed and have a desire to remove my part of it within the world.

Let's say you have one hundred beans. Ninety of them are things that feel good, ten of them are things that do not feel good. There are fifty people and all of you have the same balance, ninety/ten. All fifty people—do the math—five hundred unfortunate circumstances, and my part was my ten.

NOTE: Here is the cat now. He comes to her lap as I have

asked him to do. Why have I? To help her connection to me. Cats/felines are very good with extrapolating emotions and shifting them to a better state. For that reason, I use them often to soothe the mind of a channel.

I have no responsibility to remove my ten because I cannot remove anything. Every thought that has ever been thought remains. What I can do, however, is have an Intention to come into the world, to be faced with a situation that is similar to some extent, and guide my person to choose the opposite. In that way, I have cleared my leftover.

I am breaking it down with very elementary examples so that you understand what you call karma. It does not follow you into "heaven." It does not follow you back into your body. It is not baggage like weight or chains that follow you around until you undo it. You can never undo what you did. You cannot undo it, but you can be faced with a similar choice and redo the choice. Different time-space-reality does matter.

Can you go back in time in the nonphysical and undo that choice? Yes, you can. Does it impact the world? No, it does not. At all? No, it does not. Does it change what your choices are in the nonphysical if you clean it up in the Spirit Dimension? It can if that is what you choose to do. There are no limitations where we are and that is where I leave that because you are not destined karmatically to face obstacles in life. You choose to have an experience where you are hoping that your person does something for the benefit of all.

What are you hoping they do? Choose love, choose happy, choose joy when faced with a situation where it does not appear that love and happy and joy are plentiful. I say

Chapter 2 ~ Thoughts Create Things

specifically *does not appear* to be plentiful, but abundance *is* present. You have to soften the mind and receive it. If you allow us to, we (we, being the Guides that help you with your thought patterns), can change your thought pattern instantly.

You are a human being and you have the ability to think. You have what we call a radar within this attractor within. We also teach this as law of attraction and law of creating, because any thought that you have is drawing things to you. You are in the midst of creating something.

But what are you creating? Whatever it is that you are focused on. In a situation where something seems disastrous, if you have the presence of mind to see it from a different perspective ("I haven't done it this way before"), it is an opportunity to receive a good idea on how to handle the situation. "This is a good opportunity to walk away, I have not done that in a while. This is an opportunity to choose whether or not to engage. I have not done that one in a while"—and so on and so forth.

When you are thinking thoughts on a subject and you are off on a track that is harmful to your way of life, you know that it is true. It is harmful for the world's way of life as well. We teach you about that, many of us, because every thought that has ever been thought remains. If it is here, then more like it can accumulate. People and their internal radars can home in on it. We do not want that.

We are evolving constantly. All of the lifetimes that we have ever had continue to evolve at their own speed. If one lifetime has this ninety/ten split, that lifetime can choose to simplify their learning on those ten unfortunate circumstances and do it in the world. Simplify, because that is where the thought and the action was created. You go to the source of the activity.

Different continent does not matter; male or female different, does not matter; a thousand years later, it can matter. The only one it matters to is the Higher Self of that personality; that is the only one. That personality holds themselves back not at all.

Why does it matter to the Higher Self? We said it *matters*; we did not say they care in a negative way. They are not disappointed. But it does matter. They like all the choices that every lifetime has had. We do not make mistakes. We know the next thing that we want to do and we embark upon it. Sometimes, when we want to redo something (not undo it), we set it aside and we do a number of other things first, if that is the plan. We are not Wild Wild West, willy-nilly Beings. We are Knowledge walking.

I ask Carol often, "What is your plan today, what do you want to do today?" Most of the time, of late, she says, "I don't know, I'm really behind the curve on planning out my week. But I will sit down and I will do the work now to make sure that my day unfolds in a way that's pleasing to me." I say, "Good." She asks me how to forecast better—what to do tomorrow or the next day or the next. I tell her that we are going to get to that but right now she has too many things going on. Some of them feel good, many of them do not. So it is better to currently plan day by day.

It is a weight off her shoulders, because adding one more thing is sometimes too much. It is perceived too much, that is truth; however, sometimes it is. There is a balancing act and one thing can tip the balance. So, right now, I assure her

Chapter 2 ~ Thoughts Create Things

that there are better days coming. Things are lining up, and the more she perceives what she is wanting, the more her daily lineup consists of just those things. She understands what I mean by that, and she does the energy work to clean away the dust of some of the other things that have lined up. Life is full, life is colorful, but life can be easier.

I talk to you a little bit about law of attraction. What is it? You. Law of attraction is you. It is the inner psyche of the mind. It has evolved and we love it. We love it so much that we watch over it, we tend to it. As we do you. When I say the mind, I mean ego. We watch over and tend to the ego. It is a behavior in the world that we watch over and it manifests within the psyche of the mind of people.

That ego currently feels abandoned by God.

I am giving you the long story so you can understand what the law of attraction is, in addition to how it works so that you can cause it to work with you rather than against you. The ego and the world. It is in the world. The belief, if you prefer the word, in the world, resident in this planet, is abandonment by God. Why? Because the world evolved to believe that.

Every thought is still here. Not every thought is good, and thoughts have created a world where there is unrest, fear, and abandonment. Where did that start? A thought. A simple thought was the seedling that grew. It did not have to grow, but it did. Same for each of you. When you have a thought that does not feel good, it does not have to grow. You can learn to ignore it and focus on that which you are wanting.

The world, over time, chose to pay attention to two things: preferred and preferred not. Over time, the mind began to think on its own. Prior to that there were no thinking thoughts, there were just ideas received from Source. That was so long ago that it does not necessarily matter to each of you now, but some of you are very inquisitive and you want to know the whys, the whys, the whys.

There is an opportunity to ask more questions on that subject. Decide what you are wanting to know about it and then ask us. But, until then, this is where we begin on the subject. The mind evolved itself, and when the mind evolved itself it learned how to think. Then it learned how to realize that it was thinking on its own and limited its receiving from Source. Fast forward: it stopped listening to Source, and here you are. The mind believes that it is supposed to think and do everything for you and so it tries to.

When I say change your mind, I am talking about change what is being attracted to you from the inner-mind. You are the human being that is experiencing the life that is being manifested for you from the internal psyche of your own mind. That internal psyche is the law of attraction, because it is the attractor.

The mind itself is meant to reach out and know that there are thoughts that are helpful for the person that it is resident in the world with. An easy way of describing this is that the mind decided it no longer needed to be taught how to create vibrationally inside the world, this sub-reality. Simulating now, the mind put up a hand and said, "No more teaching, I know how to do it." Then it began to focus not on us, not on communication coming from the dimension that is Real, but instead began to simulate what it thought it was supposed to do. It is still doing that. It is identifying thoughts and ideas.

Chapter 2 ~ Thoughts Create Things

Your sub-reality, alternate realities, alternate universes—the inner psyche of the mind is unaware that they exist and unaware where it is drawing thoughts from because that is where its learning stopped. It happens every time. Every world is the same. It happens every time, but it happens in a different way. One world, the mind goes a little further and then uses telepathy specifically within itself. People are in the world, but they are within their own thought bubbles, unaware that others are too in the world. But they are creating and creating and creating and creating and doing and doing and doing many things because the mind has learned this do-loop within its own etheric field.

There are many things that go on in the mind of someone who is having an existence in a physical realm where they are the creator. They are making things and changing it and making things and changing it. Then there are worlds where the mind did not shut itself out from us completely, but it listened only partway. The instructions are then only half-heard. All of you interact with people and know what it feels like to ask someone to do something when they have only heard it partway.

It is human evolution. It is fascinating and it is normal. Your world is normal, it just evolved in a different way. How did your mind evolve? It stopped listening to us after it learned the lesson about telepathy; that once you go into the world, the mind reaches out, follows the thoughts, selects, and brings something back. This, the mind has learned extremely well. It is law of attraction! That was its last lesson, so to speak, and it has become very good at it. Now it bases what it draws to you, the human being that it is connected to (each psyche of the mind has its own person; you are a pair) what it draws to you is the last thing you thought about. Period. It does not get more complicated than that.

The simplicity is maddening because when you break it down, what was the last thing? It is a combination. The last thing is not singular. It can be an item, it can be a color, it can be several emotions, it can be an expectation, it can be a multitude of things. The psyche of the mind has learned to identify all of them and bring all of them to you.

Now, which ones do you get faster? It is an easy question. Quantity wins. Whatever you had for breakfast today, describe it, add emotional words to it as much as you can. That is what your inner attractor is currently focusing on. It also knows in the moment that you were eating your breakfast, every morsel that you enjoyed or did not enjoy. Which ones were really, really good, whether or not that was the breakfast you actually wanted or whether you sacrificed and chose second best. Whether you had no time, whether you had too much time, whether you had no money or did not care about money, whether you were indoors or outdoors, hot or cold, by yourself, not by yourself.

Your Soul Being is the one that is watching everything that is happening and directing your thoughts after the situation has occurred. In the moment that something is occurring the psyche of the mind has assumed front and center. It pays attention to everything and begins what it thinks its job is. Then, the beautiful Being that is you in the nonphysical steps in and begins pulling back, pulling back, pulling back all of the things that it does not want you to experience.

Chapter 2 ~ Thoughts Create Things

At the same time, there is you. Moving on to the next segment of your day, and it is this ongoing dance of I think, I do, I attract, we pull back. I think, I do, I attract, we pull back. I think, I do, I attract, we amplify because we do that as well. Your Guide is the backup system to your law of attraction.

That Being cannot supersede your own psyche. I say that is a law of the Universe, but it is also undesired because then your minds would shut down to communication from us and then your life experience would complete itself rather quickly.

The mind knows that we (Source Beings) are present, but it does not know that we are supposed to be doing the job that it is doing, guiding you to the next thing that you are wanting. It is easy to give you analogy after analogy, example after example. Substitute any you like. The student assuming the role of the teacher is the best one.

Are we angry at the psyche of the mind? No. As said, it happens every time. It is the process of evolution of human minds.

Why do we do it, then? Because it is one of the things that the Creators created for us to do. So we do it. Why? Because it is part of ascension. Why is there ascension? Because that is what we are made for. Why were we made? To perceive life into existence. Why did we do that? Because that is what was designed for consciousness, so that is what we do. How long do we do it? It is what we do. The air is air because that is what it is. We are consciousness, so we do not do anything that is not consciousness.

Are there other things that we could do? No because

we are what is Real. Who made us? We made ourselves. How could that be? Because it was designed that way. Who designed it? Consciousness. Where did it come from? It always has been. It always will be. There is no beginning and there is no end.

When you are in human physical form, it seems like an impossibility to grasp that concept. But it is not a concept, it is reality. When you are in the nonphysical, as soon as you complete your passage back to this dimension, you understand who you are. All of your human questions on that subject are instantly answered. One by one by one, you will understand in the world, but not until the world evolves itself. At this point in your evolution the world is not knowing how to create. The psyche of the mind is drawing things to you. You have a mind that is able to think, the psyche of the mind draws things to you based on the things that you are thinking, and you think many things at one time. You can internalize them, meaning do them on purpose.

You have a bad day. Gloss over it, paint it as a pretty picture, find something in it to focus on, and focus on that and that only. Let the rest be something that falls by the wayside. Does your psyche/attractor ignore it completely? No. But it can be so little that it makes no difference to you. Is it hard to do? Sometimes. Can you learn? Absolutely. That is what I am here for. That is what all of us have been doing for decades now—talking about law of attraction, getting you to understand that your thoughts are meaningful.

There is enough knowledge in the world about continuity of life that has no bearing on Truth. People have talked about who God is, who your Guides are, who Spirit Beings are,

Chapter 2 ~ Thoughts Create Things

who the Archangels are—giving them human names and personalities. We are no such thing. We are consciousness. But in the world, people also have belief systems, Root beliefs and Crown beliefs. I am teaching the world that we are Real, that there is a purpose for the world and there is a purpose for you in the world. You were excited to come here into this lifetime and do some things, and we want you to remain in that position about life for the entire time you are here.

We never take our eyes off of you and we are always guiding you to feel happier, excited, loving, generous, desiring communication with your Parent Soul Being and with the Guides that are watching over you constantly.

The attractor within simply does not know how to do its job yet. It stopped taking guidance and direction from us on how to do it, so now we teach it in a different way. I teach you human beings verbally, so you are educated on these things. Then the mind, the psyche of your mind, learns by way of your education.

Thoughts create things. So think the better thought. Emotions are thoughts. Emotions create more like it. Reach for the better emotion. When you reminisce about some disaster, whether it happened to you or whether it was in a movie or a television show does not matter, it is a thought. Does that mean that that thing is coming to you? It could. But you are also creating more of it in the world.

The psyche of the mind is meant to do one thing: locate, hand-select, and bring to you quickly. It guesses, makes a quick decision, and fumbles around trying to figure out how to bring it back towards you. It is immature. That is all. That is all that is going on. But you can listen to these words, you can understand them, you can pay attention to these lessons and through them; we, by way of you, can retrain your mind. One by one, two by two, ten by ten, a thousand by a thousand. It will occur because the world is here and we are here. We have always been here. When the psyche of the mind listens to us, we tell it what to bring to you, and then it does while it is doing its old pattern of behavior at the same time. That is where slowness, otherwise known as delay, comes from.

How do you ask the mind to listen to us? You meditate, then have a specific question, or specific demand, and we go to work on that. Can you make law of attraction work for you by meditating? Absolutely. Can you make law of attraction work faster for you by demanding that your Guides train your mind in a certain way? Yes, that is how you participate in re-training your own psyche. Why demand that your Guide do something for you? So it registers within the psyche of the mind to expect it. How do you know what questions to ask? Get creative. The wheels are turning for many of you.

"Should I ask you to teach my mind one subject at a time? Identify it, bring it to me, show me that I have learned it, and tell me when to go on to the next subject? Should I start small, should I start big? Where's the best place for me? Where am I in the continuum of learning when I compare myself to others?" All are good questions, except do not teach the mind that it needs to know about comparison, because that is doubt.

Can you have your mind trained by your Guides to be a better selective, object-oriented attractor? Yes. How long

Chapter 2 ~ Thoughts Create Things

does that take? It depends on how well you do it. Quieting the mind is step one. Asking something of us is step two. Focusing on it cleanly is step three. Receiving it is step four. Always. Always. Always. Always.

Get good at quieting the mind and then begin asking us for things. Quiet your mind in meditation and we will use that quiet time to help you with what you have asked for. Then just sit back and let us do it. Some things we can teach your mind in an hour, and if you meditated ten minutes at a time, well, that could be six days in a row. But if in those six days you are thinking about how difficult it is going to be for us to teach you to do that thing…you cannot possibly not see the detrimental effects of this. You have undone much of what we taught you, because at the same time you have taught the mind something else, and now there are competing demands.

Should you sit in meditation for a full hour instead? No. The mind is not quieted for that length of time. You need a quieted mind to sit at length. So what do you do? A good thirty days of ten minutes—that will do it—and keep your mind on something positive (that is step three). Ask us for it, get off the subject, move on to a happier day, happier times, happier conversation, happier place, happier thought, happier music, happier, happier, happier, happier, happier. And meditate with the intent for that thing and then watch it come to you.

It is a process that we will not change, no matter who we speak through when we teach on this subject. When we choose the words, when we speak through a human being, when we teach on this subject it is the same, no matter who. Who are we? Jeshua. Who is Jeshua? A collective of nonphysical Beings with a similar focus. What is that focus? To teach the world how to channel, ultimately, specifically through this woman. But prior to that, we have to teach you how to slow down, get you to learn about feelings and emotions, and that they matter.

If you make that important to you and you start having positive intentions for this part of your day and that part of your day on this subject or that subject, this area of your life or that area of your life, then you start seeing the results. Then you have a happy life. That is part of what we always teach. We all teach that because the world needs it, it is the starting place for the world. We need you to understand that thoughts create things and everything you think about, you get some of. What you enjoy, you get faster if you do not contradict it.

It is not hard, but it does take practice. We give you all kinds of Teachers from the nonphysical and some human, straightforward teaching is occurring as well. There are people that understand what we are saying and they have good ideas and say, "I could teach that. I have a good way of explaining that." We say, go do it! Go do it! More of that, please! But when we teach about the psyche of the mind and the worlds and consciousness and teaching the mind how to do that thing that you are wanting, well, that is our department. Carol is a trance channel. An open, full, blended, consciously-aware, verbal trance channel of the Ascended, and that makes all the difference in what and how much we can teach you.

There are plenty of people who channel, and she was

Chapter 2 ~ Thoughts Create Things

one. We knew it would come easy for her. She woke up after meditation one day, and words were being written in the air with her nose—pages and pages of words. We did that with her for a couple of days, and then spontaneously, verbal channeling. Trance channeling.

Does it occur like that for everyone? No, it does not. Why not? Because sometimes you do not know who you are and sometimes that matters. In her lifetime, this one, as this person in this body with this name Carol, it was decided that it was something that she would find her way to. Meaning her Higher Self created a Life Intention for it to occur. Now, it took her a long time, but when she found it, it was brought forward as it was Intended to do.

There are many that have similar experiences and there are thousands more who do not. Some have stayed with it and continued and learned what needed to be learned so that their mind would allow channeling. There are some as well that gave up on it. We do not want you to give up and is why we teach how to channel through her. We give you the Four Pillars so that you learn well and then you know that it is not all up to you. It is not a right-or-wrong, plus-or-minus type of environment.

We are the Teachers of it and we give you the full breadth of information so that you can stay with it. Why do we want you all to channel? Because it means that your mind is nice and quiet and soft and supple. That you can receive from us in a way where you can get verbal guidance. With channeling, we can tell you what you need to know or do instead of guessing. Clairvoyant (ocular) receiving is good, but not as good because you have to make sense of what your inner-mind is able to translate and it often is not the full message. We love all of you, but the path of least resistance to getting your life on track is learning to channel. Verbal, accurate guidance is what we are after here to help you.

There are so many things to teach you. Law of attraction is something that we touch upon here because it gives you some exposure to how creative you can get with it. Creating a list of things you want, hiding it in a drawer, and never thinking about them can still bring them to you if you are happy. They sure can. But if you give up on those things that you wrote down and put in a drawer, you talked yourself out of believing you would have them, then it is unlikely you will allow them into your life's experience. Thoughts create things.

How does the mind feel about us is where we continue after Carol has some lunch. We are Jeshua and we have enjoyed this conversation, and for now, this chapter is complete.

CHAPTER 3

Telepathy Renewed

*When the ego mind understands that we are
intelligence and not just the vibration of
thoughts that reside in the world,
that we are present and accounted for,
Real, that we are intelligence
and speaking to it, not a memory
of something that had been spoken,
it jumps for joy.*

Chapter 3 ~ Telepathy Renewed

Session: 4, video: #0019
July 17, 2021

Personal Conveyance: "*All right, we continue. Today is July 17, 2021; it is 8:51 p.m. We are here in Carol's video room in Cranberry Township, Pennsylvania and continue writing this book. We are on Chapter Three. Which book is it? The first one in a second series, Mind Body Connection. I am writing these books in the order that I want you to read them, and I do have several series that I have prepared for you.*

I do have many things to teach the world, so here is what I want to do. I am going to let you know, Carol, that it is okay to be worried. But don't be. I've got your back. There is no scribe to do this with you. Nobody to remind you when to sit down and do these pages except for me. So as we're watching the new Smallville (Supergirl) I want you to know it doesn't harm you. (Personal conversation continued on what Carol's vibration was ready to engage in specific to television. She shied away from all things violent to the point of removing joy from her life). I know you love the show. Watch it again. But as you're watching the show, I say, "Light her up!" That means for your Guide to tingle your whole body. Then you know that is us asking for your attention. Now we also said we could touch your face or pick up your hand, but I like "Light her up!" It's fun, I like to do that.

There's a lot to do. There's book-writing and there's proofing. Don't sit and watch the television all day. You don't have anybody else to do the proofing. You need to listen to the book and proof it yourself with me, out loud. It is the very best way to do it. Taxing on your time, but it is the best way. Yes, you hear me in the mind. The girls are doing a good job, but they are not you. (Carol initially asked friends to look at the transcription and correct spelling errors from the auto transcription, but it was too difficult of a job for them. They did not understand the material well enough to know where to break paragraphs, et cetera).

The publisher will fix errors in punctuation; I am not going to add all of them. Your mind is too aware of the words for me to do it that way. They aren't going to rewrite the book. I know you worry about that. They will want paragraphs and chapters complete. When you find something that does not make sense to you, ask me to read it out loud through you and you will understand more fully when I do. It is a simple shift in sentence structure with the auto transcription that is the error. We will do this together, I promise you. Omit the "ands, sos, and buts"—whatever you need to do to make the beginning of a sentence grammatically correct. You could be fast at it or slow, but I want you to be okay with reading the book, making the needed grammatical edits, and turning it in.

Carol is asking me now, "But there are so many books that have thank-yous and acknowledgements for proofing, for editing, for helping, and there is always a list of people. Do I need multiple people to proofread it? What is the right thing to do to prepare the manuscript?" You just need one, Carol—you—and then be happy with it. She's saying now, "But the difference between watching and listening to a video and reading it on paper, it's vastly different. (The auto

Chapter 3 ~ Telepathy Renewed

transcription placed numerous errors in paragraphing and sentencing. It bothered her to an incredible degree.) How do I make it correct by myself? How do I clean the energy up of being afraid to do it?" (I told her we will do it together, but even with her abilities she was unsure that I could do it through her without a scribe. I assured her it is good the way I wrote it. It is, and I hope you enjoy it.)

Let's continue. Dictation begins now - Chapter Three.

People have a habit of thinking about the same thing time and time and time again. When they do, they curse the world because they get something that they were afraid of. Then they become afraid that they are going to get it again. It becomes a cycle. We want the cycle to stop. We want people to understand what telepathy is. Telepathy is not bad, but right now it is not altogether good either. It is incomplete. In this world, it is incomplete.

Consider this: a rocket scientist entered third grade and halfway through decided he/she no longer wanted to learn from the teacher, that they understood rockets well enough. They stopped listening; they turned the corner and just began doing something that had to do with rockets, believing all the while that they had already learned everything they needed to about rockets. Convincing that person that they did not, in fact, learn everything about rockets and had barely begun their training is rather difficult because they turned the corner. We know exactly where they are in their training, but they do not.

We know where you are. Your interior mind does not know where we are. It looks around the universes, finding things to bring to you because it thinks that that is its job.

In fact, it is, but it never learned how to do its job and just began climbing the ladder of sophisticated delivery. Only it is like the movie *Groundhog Day*—it climbs two rungs and starts again, climbs two rungs and starts again, climbs two rungs and starts again. It does not know any more than the beginning.

It is a program that is on a loop and it keeps looping back to the beginning. There is nothing else there for it to do. It did not progress because it did not listen. As I have said, it happens every time. It is what the mind does. Why do we not fix the mind? We do, after it makes the error. It is part of life in the worlds. It is experiencing the error and then the error is corrected.

Now, the error—Carol wants to capitalize it. I am okay with her capitalizing it because I know that she knows what "the error" means. I do not want it capitalized because I do not want the mind to take in that it did something special and continue doing so.

I will explain. The mind knows "different" equals "special," meaning something it should take notice of based on emphasis. Emphasis in the written word is not just bold, underlined, italic, quotes, or whatever fancy way you have of aligning words on a page. It is a capital letter. A capital means the beginning. So I do not ask for the words "the error" to be capitalized, but I explain to you that it could easily be substantiated to have it written that way.

The mind takes in everything it sees, so I say little "e" error, which means turn a blind eye to it. Look away, look away, look away, do not do it again. It minimizes the effect while I explain what happened to the inner-mind, to you, the reader—your ears, your eyes. You take in the meaning, and you understand the meaning, most of you, but the eyes takes in the capitalization, which has another meaning altogether.

The mind does eventually become aware that we are here because the human being is taught continuity of life in one fashion or another, religion mostly. It is not the only way, however. People talk about simple things as well, such as red cardinals—"I know it is my parent saying hello to me." Or, "I was just thinking about you and then a butterfly threw itself into my window. That also happened on the day you passed so I know it is you. Don't do that anymore, though, because I care about the butterfly."

Now, how does the second scenario mean continuity of life? Because a human being is still talking to a Loved One in their mind. It is a one-way conversation, but they are assuming that this poor butterfly was driven into a window so that the human being would know that his/her Loved One did not die. That would never happen. It cannot because we never harm life. That includes a butterfly.

The story the inner-mind takes in is about God and the disasters that he allowed or initiated or supported or influenced or was proud and happy of. These are the worst stories that were ever created because the mind learned something about God: that God does not love what he created. The interior mind says, "Who is it that I feel then, present always? There is always the presence of love. There is always a presence of love. I thought that was God."

I am talking about the interior mind. How does the interior mind always say this? Because it knows that we are always here. We are the ones that helped you move into the earth plane, and we remain with you always. We light up the chakras and we keep them going and we do hundreds of other things for your physical body. In addition, all the things that we do to draw things to you that are pleasing for what you were wanting, and for what your Parent Soul Being is wanting.

When the mind woke up as you were born, our presence was already there. Consecrated life means consciousness was brought within the human physical form. It was at that time, whenever that moment-point was, that the mind began to think. From the moment it is able to think, it is able to remember. That moment is generally at birth; it can be sooner, rarely later.

We are Real. We bring your portion of the greater part of you into the earth plane, into your physical form, then we turn your chakras on, your energy field, the etheric layers that surround you. Then your mind clicks on. It is the way life begins. When the mind clicks on, we are already there. It has never lived even a microsecond without us. It is aware of our presence. It is aware because we have always been there, so we are—the amount that it pays attention to us—normal, because we have always been there.

The body knows it has a nose because it has always been there. By the time the mind is aware of anything, it is already there. Same thing, although the mind cannot be aware until we click it on. But it is the same difference—the mind has awareness of us always. It has never not known the presence of us.

What it does not know is what we do for it; we keep the chakras going, we align, and attune them frequently. We invigorate the physical body. We cleanse the portion of the energy field that is desired by the Higher Self.

Why do we not cleanse the whole body? Because it would make the point of human physical life moot. There are Intentions (capital I) to be experienced. Understanding life, living and making decisions because of it, finding what you prefer, and finding the happiest things in life could not be done if we took every experience away from your etheric field. There would be no difference between nonphysical life and physical life. We like the difference. We enjoy experiencing the difference. We enjoy not the separation.

We do want people in the human physical form to better understand what this connection is supposed to be between Spirit Guide and human being.

You come into the world, you have things to accomplish, and then you find things that you want to do or have or be. Your High Guide is the most powerful Being that you are born with. I have gone over this again and again in so many different ways. The human being has a Guide and is meant to ask for verbal guidance all along this path called life. The human population is starting to get it. There are psychic medium tarot readers on almost every corner. Problem with that is many of them use intuition far too much, go telepathic/psychic far too much, ask incomplete questions far too much, provide their own description and add their own experience far too much.

Experiential descriptions from a clairvoyant medium to the person that they are trying to help is unprofessional. The human being is putting their own opinions into the reading. Now, they do not mean to, they just do not have a complete verbal picture. They convey what they have understood—clear cognizance, poor choice in words. It is not knowing; it is clear assumption. The human mind disregards the message, combines it with its own thoughts, and then presents it to the person as a knowing. A heavy weighted thought without a voice or an image to go with it, and the human being says, "It's a feeling that I have, it's so strong, and this is what it is." They emphasize *is* and we say, no, it is an assumption.

It is a best guess (sometimes it is simply a guess, not even a best one), because the human being—many of you know this—silence scares the hell out of you. When you are giving a reading to someone and they sit silent, fear creeps in. You do not want to be wrong, so you fill in the gap of silence with more words, and those words come from you, not from your Spirit Guide. Unprofessional. Strong choice of words, I know. But when you equate it to some other career path it would be the right choice. And it is the right choice, otherwise I would have chosen something else.

We teach how to channel because it is the most advanced. Every trance channel does not do it for a living but their inner-mind is the most gentled. It is soft, it is supple, it is quieted. The inner psyche of the mind is what I am referring to. In order to be a full and open trance channel, the inner-mind must understand where it is getting its information from—us.

The mind, like I said, is aware that we are present with it. There has not been a second of its life when it did not know there was a second vibration felt. One is of the world, and one is us. Why is it different? Because we are purity of love, and the world is the earth plane—dense, deep,

Chapter 3 ~ Telepathy Renewed

dark feelings, thoughts, actions. We are not that. The inner workings of the mind feels two things: beautifully peaceful, gentle, and then everything else. Only the inner workings of the mind does not know that beautiful, peaceful, gentle is also intelligence.

It knows the world is the world at large. It thinks that we are part of it; we are not. We wait until you, beautiful human beings that you are, find your way to some bookstore and you are casually browsing, not thinking a whole lot, not a lot on your mind, and we guide you to a book on astrophysics, mindfulness studies, affirmations, a coloring book for adults, the section for journals, pretty pens, bookmarks, the coffee shop, little trinkets to see what will spark your interest.

We are not the ones that guide you to anything that causes you to be afraid. What causes you to be afraid is different for every person. Your Spirit Guide knows you inside and out. If you have a fear of cooking, they will keep you far away from the cooking aisle. Why would you be afraid of cooking? Maybe you had a childhood experience where a fly fell into your soup and it grossed you out and part of you hates cooking because of it.

There is no telling how things lodge themselves in the mind because every mind is different. But if that were you, your Spirit Guide—through your intuition, a quiet nudge, the little whisper that comes from us—guides you to a different aisle. The attractor within, however, it knows that a bookstore includes cooking and, if you have had a day when you stubbed your toe or you keep looking at your nails that are overdue to get polished, or had an argument—it could block our guidance out and take you past the cooking aisle instead.

Now, if you burned your toast, forgot to eat your breakfast and your stomach is grumbling, it might beeline you to the cooking aisle as well. Who wins? Depends on how quiet your mind is. Simple as that. If your thoughts are racing, if you are a person that has convinced yourself that you just cannot sit still, you have a thousand different things flying through your mind, you will end up in the cooking aisle.

If you go to the bookstore simply to relax the mind and you walk in, breathe a sigh of relief, there is a weight off your shoulder just by stepping foot into the building—then you might hear us.

We take a backseat to the mind because the mind shoves its hand in our face, more or less. A more descriptive explanation for you is this: the mind is simply not knowing that we are intelligence, so it is not paying attention to us. It is paying attention to the world at large. It does not dismiss us on purpose, it does not ignore us on purpose. How many of you have had the experience of sitting and reading an article and someone walks in the room and they, after a time, say, "Hey." You look up and they say, "Well, what do you think?" You say, "I don't know, were you talking to me? I didn't hear you," because you can block someone out completely. Does it mean that they were not talking? No. It means you did not hear them. It means your focus was elsewhere.

That is what happens. The mind gets hyper-focused on some thing or many things. When you slow the mind down it has less things to think about. It has less things to keep track of. It is not maxed-out and then it hears us tell it to take you to the other side of the bookstore and then you do

Chapter 3 ~ Telepathy Renewed

not see cooking books.

Now, you might not register fear or fright from seeing a cookbook, but the interior of your mind spikes and that spike is unwellness. Period.

What is unwellness? Anything unwanted. It means the mind has noticed something that it does not prefer. Every time the mind notices something that it does not prefer, it brings it to you. Not only that, but after a time that thing that it does not prefer starts to accumulate. When it accumulates, it becomes a problem. Then it becomes a big problem and then it becomes a block. Then you know it is a problem because it is a habit that you cannot get rid of or a sister that keeps stealing things from you but nobody else. Behaviors, as well as situations, is what we are talking about.

You do create your own reality. There are ways to untrain the mind from what it has been doing to you. I want you to know that the body plays a part. The body, not the brain, the body. How does it play a part? Because there is more to it than you can see with your own physical eyes.

Many people around the world are teaching about wellness, about deliberate creation, law of attraction, mind over matter, that words matter, and think before you speak, as well as things like energy fields. The information that we talk about through Carol is not new to the world, although some of it is. We teach it so that you have our Knowing about it and not colorful, watered-down, or altogether inaccurate word-of-mouth type of explanations that come from people.

That sounds very critical against people, but it is not. It is simply fact. The world makes things up. You do not know what you do not know. You learn, and if you like what you learn you reteach it. As you reteach it, you twist it a little here, a little there, trying to explain it more, better, different—sometimes to explain it to yourself to understand it better. When you think you have understood it, you believe you are ready to explain it to another, but truly you never understood it to begin with. So now you are sharing misinformation. There is a plethora of misinformation on every subject that you teach each other.

When we speak through a human being we tell you one thing: Truth. If you do not like this book, if it causes you to be angry, I suggest that you put it down, take a walk and then pick it back up. The mind does know how to absorb information and I know how to teach your mind what we need it to know so that it softens and can hear us better. As a result, your intuition gets stronger and more things that you are wanting magically appear. You will be in the right place at the right time more frequently. For some of you, that will be enough.

When the mind figures out that we are intelligence, it is as if it jumps for joy because it is no longer alone, doing everything for you. It thinks it is a one-man ship, a one-man show, a captain without a crew. When it understands that we are intelligence and not just the vibration of thoughts that reside in the world; that we are present and accounted for, Real; that we are intelligence and speaking to it, not a memory of something that had been spoken, it jumps for joy. Then it wants to pay attention to us and good things start happening to you because of it.

We want you to want more than what you have today. That is what you have come here to do. To find a way to want

Chapter 3 ~ Telepathy Renewed

more of one thing—everything else is secondary. The one thing is for your inner-mind to align itself with us. How does it align itself with us? It registers within that we are alive.

The things that the mind brings to you are thoughts. When those thoughts draw closer to you, you have an experience. But it is a thought that is being drawn to you. That thought becomes refreshed as a new thought, which you experience.

Let's say you see two people holding hands. The experience began because there was a thought at some point of love (by you). There was an original (for the sake of teaching this example) thought about a man and woman being together; there was a thought about holding hands; there was a thought about walking in the park; there was a thought about having an umbrella because it is raining or too sunny; there was a thought about going outside and seeing what the weather was like; and then you see two people walking, holding hands. The mind knows what you have read or listened to or thought about and then it draws it to you.

"Where is that gosh-darn umbrella? I have lost three of them this week." Then you go outside and get rained on. Bingo. Your previous thoughts about umbrellas or rain or missing things or being in an awkward position was brought to you—in this case, as an umbrella, or the lack of one. We are not a thought. We are alive. We are Real. We are communicating with the inner-mind. Nothing else is communicating with it.

It is like walking into a library—you can read all the books, but none of the books speak to you. None of them jump off the shelf and walk over to you and sit you down and have a conversation with you. None of them have a voice, none of them have intelligent words that they are conveying to you. Thoughts are not alive. We are.

When the mind wakes up, it simply says, "Hello." We say hello back and it says, "Whoa, were you talking to me?" We say, *Yes.* It says, "How did you do that?" We say, *I can teach you.* It says, "Okay, how about now?" We say, *Okay.* It says, "Gotta go, my person needs me," and that is when a fly lands on you, when your child runs into the room, when the phone rings, when that email comes in—distraction, in other words.

Once the mind knows that we are Real, your life changes in ways that are positive. It cannot *not* happen. We want a conversation with the mind and when it stops and listens to us, we give it love. We give it love and we give it guidance based on whatever you, the human being, is wanting to experience, as well as things the Higher Self of you wants to experience through you. Co-creation at its best. Co-creation—you and us together.

We teach the mind how to bring specific things to you when you become interested in us. One by one, we continue where we left off with training the mind how to use telepathy by hearing us ocularly. We teach the mind to draw specific things to you and on purpose.

The energy field around the human being is real, and there is a lot of good information out in the world on it. Everything you teach each other is not altogether wrong, but there are some things that we correct. You find our material and either believe it or you do not but, either way, we put it out into the world again and again and again until more of you get the bigger picture.

Chapter 3 ~ Telepathy Renewed

We teach how to channel through Carol, and we bring in the Four Pillars of Learning. These are four areas that we find to be the most important things to teach you as it relates to communicating with us. The Foundational Material and who we are, law of attraction and deliberate creating, the energy field and how to self-heal, and intuitive development.

Having the suite of material that covers those four areas, you can be dumb as a bag of rocks but you are still going to get it eventually because it makes sense; it adds logic.

The energy field around you is where telepathy resides. It is also where all of your thoughts reside. When you have a bad day, your energy gets foggy, not depleted. We are not talking about your physical energy; we are talking about how crisp and clean the inner layers of the energy field are. You can fix many things that are going wrong in your life, as well as your physical body, by understanding how to direct energy within. It is like magic.

We agree with those human teachers that describe that there is life after life. Not only are we proof of it, but we created it. Who better to teach you how to communicate with us, than us? We are the Teachers of how to do it. We are the Teachers in the nonphysical dimension, and we teach other nonphysical Beings how to communicate with people from dimension to dimension, from the nonphysical to physical. We are the Teachers.

We have gone to school for these things and have become Teachers. After you Transition, should you desire to communicate with someone in the physical world and do not yet know how to do it, we teach you or your High Guide teaches you based on where you are in your ascension. We teach those Soul Beings how to part the energies and how to send their own thoughts. We also speak through people like this woman and we educate you, the human population.

We want you to understand that we are alive. We are busy keeping you alive, keeping you safe, keeping you disinterested in bad people and bad subjects, bad experiences. Keeping you hopeful, generous, kind, open-minded, communicative, happy, joyful, and in love with the right people (meaning other happy people, those that appreciate you).

On a more serious note, we teach you how to quiet the mind. Why? It is good for you, what you can do with it. We will remind you often that we are the ones that train the inner psyche of the mind so that it can show you what it has learned. Then, by law of attraction, you suddenly get more things that you are wanting. But you also get communication with your Loved Ones. So many of you are missing them and they are wanting to talk to you. They are wanting to continue with you in the way that we all do—guiding you, conversing with you, explaining things to you.

Every Loved One that has made their Transition knows all things. Their perspective is of the world as well as the nonphysical dimension. They wake up in "heaven" and suddenly know everything about everything. They know who you are and they know everything about you. They know what their interaction with you did to you or for you. They know where you are headed and they know what you are wanting. They know what your Intentions were when you came into your life and they know what you need.

We love when people ask for readings, but we do not

Chapter 3 ~ Telepathy Renewed

want people to believe in readings that are inaccurate. They cause you to suffer even more. The mind and the body are meant to work together. The body is the etheric field and the physical form. The mind is consciousness that is having a physical life experience.

End here, please. Chapter Three, complete.

CHAPTER 4

Taking of the Baton

*Every mind can be taught meditation.
There is always a way.
We do not give up on you,
so do not give up on yourselves.*

Chapter 4 ~ Taking of the Baton

Session: 5, video: #0678
November 12, 2021

Twice now, I have written books about consciousness, about things that matter from our perspective. Twice now I have written books that you have in your hands. You have no idea how many times I or others like me have given this information to the world—how the mind works, how the aspects of the mind come together to form your personality.

I tell you this so that you know that you are not really here. I tell you this so you have an understanding that we are Real. I tell you this because the mind has forgotten. I do love this topic. I do love the world, so I do love you. I do love life. I do love angling into the world and moving out of the worlds. I do it with ease every time I do it. When do I do it? When the need arises. But I do not do it in the old ways, having to be birthed by a mother. I simply walk through the dimensions and become whomever it is that I intended to be.

I could come in any age, either sex, any height, any weight, any stature—with no birth certificate to account for my having been in the world. True or false? It is true. I write in plural at times because there are many at my level and we do the same things when it comes to teaching you.

When we do step in it is always on purpose. It is always for a reason. It is always at our own choosing. Generally, we do it because there is a need; however, we can do it whenever we like because we know how to. We may want to invigorate the energies of a lifetime of our own and do it by stepping back into the world. We do not do this when that human being (assuming we are recreating the bodily form that we had) has family members and people that knew us still in the world and could identify the dead man walking. We do not scare people.

The example is simply to tell you that we can. We do not resurrect the body, dig it up, patch it together, solidify it, and then step in as though it is a suit to be worn. We do not have need of those theatrics because we are creators. We are exquisite at what we do.

How do we create? We have a thought. We weave the energies together. We draw from others if we need to and then we have it. We have the form or the moment or the opportunity or the environment because we have created it. You, Spirit Beings, incarnate are somewhat immature in how you go about creating. You create by way of evolution in the world. Evolution in the world are thoughts that have created your environment and this world has been here far longer than you could even perceive.

The thoughts that have accumulated over time have created the world that you have now, as well as the experiences of anyone before you. In this particular earth or world, you are born from the female sex of the human being. DNA has nothing to do with it, but evolution has taken its course. If you are not a step-in then you become an infant by way of the mother's womb. The way the mother receives the fetus within is very well known to be intercourse. Male to female intercourse. A fetus is created and then we wait for the timing to be as was planned, and then the beautiful, glorious Spirit Being who plans to become that child of the parents will move into position to assume the flesh of the body.

Chapter 4 ~ Taking of the Baton

When they move into position is at the discretion and the decision of the Being that is planning to become that person. If they want memory of the birthing process to any degree, then it is while the child is still in utero. If they do not want memory of the birthing process, physical human memory, then they breathe life of consciousness within that fetus moments before the child has completed the birthing process—their coming into the world. Consciousness is deposited within at the discretion of the Soul Being that has identified with Intentions to live life as the person that that fetus will become.

Why do I start here? It must seem random to you. I assure you, it is not. There is so much pain and suffering in the world. There is so much that you do not know, and there are so many heartbroken parents and grandparents that do not understand that life is meant to be lived and the duration of which is not always old age.

We are not careless in the decisions that we make. There are certain things that we must experience. The death of a child is not something that you must experience or else. But we must experience the birthing process a number of times and, if we choose to, a number of ways. There is value in it to that Parent Soul Being that each of you have. It is part of growing into an Ascended Being.

Love is weaved in. Love is incarnate. Love is all there is. I know I come through to Carol as a rowdy man, with a deep tone sometimes, a decision-maker. I have the persona of a gentleman, yet masculine. It is a persona to connect with her. She finds me funny. Do know this: I am not a man. I am not a woman either. I am also not, not alive. I am very much alive, as are you. In the physical and the nonphysical, you are having a dual life experience.

One by one, by one, by one, this human race will begin to understand that you are having a life experience in a physical world. It is meant to be good. It is meant to be pleasing and connected to that Parent Soul Being so that it can guide you. This is a textbook in action. Life is not flippant, casual, a toss of the dye get-what-you-get, pick up the pieces and deal with Karma. It is not like that at all. The world has evolved into a place where we do things multiple times in order to get them done simply because you human beings, we love you so much, do not stay connected to your Source.

That is why I teach the Unfoldment. It is why we, as Jeshua, teach intuitive studies. So that we can train you and we can educate you on who we are, why you all ought to have communication with us, not dole out your dollars by tens or twenties or hundreds to have a reading by a practitioner. You should all be sitting in the morning receiving guidance on your upcoming day.

Morning guidance might go something like this: "This is what is coming up for you, we are with you. It is going to be a glorious day, no matter what. If you run into trouble and emotions start to erupt, pause, breathe, step back, and let's have a brief conversation. Then re-engage. If you find yourself having to engage rapidly, you have missed the opportunity to step back. Don't walk about slowly, but do pay attention to your emotions. For it is in the emotions that I will be with you."

That is how life was meant to be lived: guided by your emotions, and if you run into trouble perceived or real, stop,

Chapter 4 ~ Taking of the Baton

get further guidance. Continue. Run into trouble, perceived or real, stop, receive further guidance, and be on your way.

You are meant to be guided through life in the physical world, but the way this human race has evolved you believe that you are here on your own. So much so that the entire mind is clouded and cannot see or hear or feel us. The inner-mind, (the ego mind) has drafted a new plan, shut the door on the Guide in favor of being in control. The inner-mind receives no guidance. It is an attractor and it simply scans the world, believes that whatever you have the most of in thoughts and emotions is what it should bring more of to you. And so it does.

The inter-mind has a different plan. It moves about holding hands with its greater Being, experiences life, stays on the path. It is an angel whispering in your ear. It is not just a metaphor. It is whispering in your metaphoric ear. We want you all to be verbal receivers of guidance. If all you can muster is some physical sensations, we will take it. Your life would be better for it if you received verbally, as well as any other ocular activity, but all forms are good. It is all purposeful. It is all extraordinary. It is all a testament to your own willingness to sit and allow us to teach the inner-mind.

We break this down for you. Parent Soul Being—your super-conscious self and the "You" in the nonphysical. The consciously-aware you—the egoic self, the part of you that is "physically focused" on your life's experiences. It is the "you" that you are aware of. Then the sub-conscious you—the unconscious part of your super-conscious self while you are in physical form (inner-mind). It is the part of you that thinks that it is supposed to bring life to you based on quantity. It is the part of you that shut down learning and became unable to do all things it was supposed to do—it is unconsciously aware that it is a nonphysical entity. Lastly, the Spirit within (inter-mind). It is not dormant, but also does not have clean, clear receiving from its greater Being. What it does receive is emotional guidance.

The inner-mind (the sub-conscious mind and egoic self) scans this physical, vibrational world for all things that pertain to it. When the inter-mind, the Spirit within, receives intuited guidance, the inner-mind knows it because it scans its own environment and the inter-mind is part of its environment.

Picture a bully who is standing in front of a person. That person is the most gentle, beautiful, intelligent, creative, artistic, athletic being that there could possibly be. The bully stands right in front of it and says, "No, I block your path. You cannot decide what happens today. That's my job." Now, the bully is not mean, but it believes that it has a job to do because the human mind has evolved in that way. It did not mean to take over a job that was not meant for it. It does not have brash, egotistical, angry sentiments. It simply took the baton. It took the baton and is using it and figured out what it thought it was supposed to do with it. The baton would have been given to the inter-mind, had it learned properly.

It was never meant to take the baton, but life in every world evolves similarly. Recourse is that we set the world on a course for the inner-mind to hand the baton back to the inter-mind. Then the floodgates open. Verbal communication, creativity as well as feelings of joy, abound.

You are all in the world at a certain point in time, in

Chapter 4 ~ Taking of the Baton

this lifetime. Save a few of you, you have been here many times before. There will always be young ones, newbies, but it is best if we generalize here. You have all been here before and you have aided the world. You have included your lives as part of the history of the world—the physical world. We are not talking about the Akashic. We are talking about your physical world.

You have accumulated experiences in past lives that have helped to evolve the world. Every lifetime has not stuck its middle finger up at everyone and created hate and discontent. Some lives have been very peaceful and they have attempted to create balance.

That is good.

That is what we are all meant to do, have peaceful lives. Move about, experience things, stay connected, push a little here, push a little there, learn something, help someone, and be guided. You are a perceived human being that is asking itself what it should do in any given situation.

When we talk about the Parent Soul Being, we do tend to describe it as though it is a different Being. It is not. Some of you are ready for this. Some of you will learn it here and now. You are the greater Being that you will go back to. You are the one that decided to be a person and the greater part of you is guiding you. It is truly the you-not-you, the nonphysical to the physical. It is you in perfect balance between the worlds. You are steady here and your physical body is intact. At the same time you are steady there, in the nonphysical world where all thought begins.

Ideas originate somewhere and then something is created. What things? Everything. We then breathe life to an idea.

We breathe love to it. Then it grows and becomes more until we decide to do something with it.

Every simulation is thought about first. Every sub-reality is thought about first. We say "create" for we create with our minds. We create with energies. We create using creativity and creativity is thoughts formed together to be the thing that we were wanting.

You began life as who you are before you entered into this world as an infant. There was a plan. Life as you did not begin the moment that your Soul Being squeezed through the veil, found your body, and clung to it. Your life began when you, that nonphysical Being that you are, decided that it wanted to have another lifetime. Then it built-in all kinds of things. It identified where first, which continent, and then narrowed down from there. That is how life begins. It begins before it starts. There is always a beginning before the beginning. And so it is.

This material is added here to remind you that you are consciousness Beings. You are meant to have a life that is happy and joyful and full of love, creativity, and the like. You are not meant to argue and fight, disintegrate things, beat people up, including yourself. You are not meant to experience retrograde and things falling apart—relationships included.

The world evolved into a place where human beings decided they wanted to build on the land, using the land. You used your natural resources, you used your eyeballs and you said, "I can use that. The clay, it sticks together. I can build a hut or that cavern in the rock. I could live there."

You cannot possibly understand how life evolved, nor for

Chapter 4 ~ Taking of the Baton

how long it has been evolving. At no time do we imply that this world is useless or that people have failed. You have evolved nicely because you are here. We watch the world at large and when the world needs our help, we provide it—and that has occurred on a number of occasions. The world is undergoing a shift currently as this book is being written. Waves of photon energy are being brought into the world in concentrated amounts and then unleashed to help heal the world.

Now, if you are religious, you will put a spin on it that is not meant to be there. If you are new-agey, you might get it. If you are in love with Source, it will begin to make sense. You will still put your own imagery to it, which will be incorrect—and we have assisted in that bad imagery—but we do need to use your language and describe who we are.

The way we have described it through Carol is that we are the ascended Ones, that we have learned everything about everything—and we have. We have identified levels and we have talked about them before. They are not true levels, but they are nevertheless learning areas. Once you have completed your learning areas, you have become an ascended.

We have described these levels from two to ten, and then we skipped to twelve. We identified eleven as Christing. Carol said, "Well, what is Christing? Is that the Jesus entity?" We said "No, it is altogether separate, however, we do say Christing because it is the name that you use, that you associate with the one known as Jesus, Jesus Christ, Jesus the Savior. So we say elevens are Christing because they are the saviors."

Carol asked, "Does that mean they are the healers and twelves are the teachers?" We said, "You're learning a little bit. You're incorrect, but you are learning." She said, "Say more," as she always does and we described that eleven is not a level but an activity that the twelves do.

When the twelves form together to do a certain activity, they always have a choice of whether to participate (this is how we put it in the beginning) and then they form their energies together. They create an energy orb that is then angled through the dimensions, into the world and then is opened. The energies of Source are then unleashed.

It took some time—months of this conversation—before Carol piped up and said, "Why would any of the twelves say no?" Then it was months again before she said, "There are no limitations, though, and everybody (nonphysical Beings) knows what you're doing. Is it allowed for someone who's not a twelve to decide that they want to do an eleven activity and then do it?" We said, "Well, yes, you can and yes, they have. Then she said, "So it's not an activity that the twelves do." We said, "It is, because we formed the idea, but it is an activity that all are welcome to join." There she paused because she was still putting pieces together.

The point is, she learns from us. We like that.

Because—listen to the words—she learns *from* us, not learns *about* us. Learns from us! That is special, indeed.

It is good to have communication with your Guide. It is good to have accurate conversation with your Guide. Your half of the bargain is always accurate because you know what you are saying. You might be misguided or incorrect, but you know what you are sending. You do not know what

Chapter 4 ~ Taking of the Baton

you are receiving. It is gobbledygook to the mind until it is love shared using words that the mind can understand and translate and then provide to you. There is a process.

Every person is slightly different because one mind may eat it up and want conversation from the pure tone that we are. Other minds are very fixated on the world, and they only give half a glance to that pure tone as it is coming in. Meditation heals all things, including the inner-mind. It is accidental, the snatching of the baton. If the inner-mind had an opportunity to receive a lesson from us then it would sit quietly because it enjoys the soothing nature of what we feel like. It is a tone that is felt, reverberated throughout the body, and the inner-mind says, "Oh, whatever that is, it feels good."

Repetition. You sit quietly. Soothing tone is felt. You stop sitting quietly, the worldly tone is felt. Far different. When you do that over and over and over and over, the mind puts two and two together. Then it wants you to slow down. It makes time for you to meditate. It dissuades you from being involved in competition on every level. *It wants us.* You become a peaceful person who does not feel good in unpeaceful environments. That is when the inner-mind has decided that it likes conversation with us. Then the lessons begin.

Meditate and then...how long does it take? It is different for every person. The stubbornness of the inner-mind is different for every person. The mind wants to run around, play games, talk to people, work, fix things, find solutions, build things, vegetate in front of the television, worry— which includes praying for most of you.

There are peaceful ones, and there are peaceful ways that you are teaching each other. We applaud you. But the mind is busy, that is the point. The mind is thinking and then you are the do-er of its thoughts. Some minds think constantly—others, more intermittently.

People who cannot sit down—they interrupt, they always have a smart aleck comment, they always have to know who is doing what and when, they jump in where they do not belong, they do not listen. That is an exterior behavior of the inner-mind, and it is stronger on the inside. If you know a person with attention-deficit-like behaviors, the inner-mind takes more effort to teach how to become quiet.

Every mind is different; however, every mind can be taught through meditation. When we talk to you one-on-one, we guide you specifically. For example, "For you, you are at nine and a half minutes. Just round it to ten and you'll be fine. Ten minutes of meditation every day, and this is what it should be like for you." Or, "Okay, for you, you are a three. No worries, three is better than two and two is better than needing jumping jacks before meditation."

There is always a way, people. There is always a way. We do not give up on you, so do not give up on yourselves. There are things that we want you to know and some of those things are in this book. This is book two. Read them in that order. On purpose, they were written. There are several series of books and they are written in such a way to invigorate the ability of the inner-mind to learn.

If you have come upon this book without reading the first one, *Ocularity of the Mind*, it is recommended that you hold onto this one and begin with the first book. Your mind

Chapter 4 ~ Taking of the Baton

will thank you for it.

There will be some of you that continue anyway. It is simply that by the time you finished the books, more would be understood by the inner-mind when read in order. You will have advanced its willingness to partner with us so that your mind can be taught easier to hear us clean, clear, and accurate. Nevertheless, do as you will; we love you no matter what.

End chapter.

CHAPTER 5

Refinement

*You get to decide what you will do,
how you will do it, how well you will do it,
when you will do it, if you will do it.
You are the doer. You are the thinker.
You are the motion-activated life.*

Chapter 5 ~ Refinement

Session: 6, video: #0679
November 2, 2021

You have a say in what you do in this lifetime, both before you come into the body and while you are in it. Most of you focus on the things that you, the physical human being, is wanting only. You do not know or you do not give a hoot about what those other things were that you Intended to do. Whether or not you decide to ease into your life or to come charging in is up to you. The way you play and live your life, your behaviors, your mannerisms, come from what you are doing to yourself, mostly.

If you decided to ease into life and have this peaceful way then it will be harder for you to be somebody that takes life by the horns and forces things to happen. If you are pushed into that kind of lifestyle, you will accumulate inter-stress, as well as inner-stress.

Inter-stress means that you have things to undo. Inner-stress is the type of stress that you know of that accumulates and manifests as something undesirable.

We do want you to know what you are doing to your lives. There are ways of relieving stress. There are ways of deciding how to interact with people. You teach yourselves and each other how to behave, how to be active listeners, how to sit quietly and pay attention, how to be kind and courteous, to say please and thank you—gentleness. Many of the things that you teach each other, you believe that you should.

No matter what, we love you and we have a desire for you to be healthy physically. When you are opposite of who you meant to be, you experience struggle and you manifest struggle, and you make struggle. When you decide to do something, you get to decide how you will do it—with anger, with joy, with fortitude, bells and whistles, fanfare, minimum, or none at all. You get to decide what you will do, how you will do it, how well you will do it, when you will do it, if you will do it. You are the doer. You are the thinker. You are the motion-activated life.

But you do not understand that you create your lives. You do not understand that you, in this moment, are creating the future you in this lifetime. So what do you want to create? Wealth? How about wealth plus an AND. Wealth and a fancy car. All right, keep going. Wealth and a fancy car and a house. Wealth and a fancy car and a big house. Wealth and a fancy car and a grand estate, not a house.

You went from home to a big home to a grand estate. Those words to you individually are different from each other—you get the gist of it—that is refinement of ideas. We want you to have things. We do not want you to be spiritual puppets walking around in robes and feeling the emotions, as well as the weight of the world. We want you to jump out of bed, skip around and love your life—make things, do things, have things. But do it with peace and joy and happiness, not only for yourself, but for everyone that you come into contact with.

If you are practicing the ways of mindfulness, then you are simply choosing to home in on the peacefulness part first. If you are jumping into life and decisions and making things happen and you make no time for meditation or even soothing activities—quiet evenings with a loved one or by

Chapter 5 ~ Refinement

yourself, a roaring fire and your dog or cat at your feet—then you are simply starting with the what and not the how.

It is a choice. Either one will do. We want to teach you to do both. There is no sacrifice of one over the other. It is always desired that you have AND. When you add the AND, you get more of whatever it is that you were wanting. It is the way of it. When you have happy, pleasing thoughts, emotions follow. When happy meets happy it amplifies, it magnifies, and you are the recipient of it. The mind thinks and thinks and thinks and thinks, it gathers and gathers and gathers and gathers, it collects and collects and collects and collects.

It simply gives you whatever it has the most of in random ways. It has a lot of frustration—so you lose your keys, you get a bad grade, you get lost, you get confused, you thought you had enough money and do not. There are limitless ways that the mind can bring you frustration. Swap frustration for any other emotion. We want you to forecast your life in a way that says, "I love my life, I love everything about my life, I always have." Then fill in the blank with something that you adore. "I always have money. I always have friends. I always have great ideas. I always have..."

When you figure out that you get to have things, then you start going after them. That is where most of you are because you teach each other you have to be this, you ought to be that, make sure you do this, not that. You have a way of accidentally-on-purpose pushing each other into lifestyles and ways of being that are unhealthy.

We do love you and we do love life. We do not love what you are doing to the world. The way most of you make your decisions is by pressure, influence. You are not deciding what you want nor how you want to go about getting the thing that you want. Far too many of you are in jobs, in relationships, or homes that you do not want. You either did not want it outright or it was more subtle—a feeling of indecision or fear.

Fear accumulates and then it manifests in not-so-mysterious ways. Some of you bright people have started tracking these things and you have come up with some identifiers, triggers—do not do this, for it is likely to manifest more of what you have found because your attention is on it. We say, however, "Well done" when you are correct with your research.

You do not need to be stressed. You simply need to make a different choice. That choice needs to be one that involves kindness to yourself. If you are kind to a human being out of obligation then you are falsely kind and also unkind. Falsely kind to the other, and unkind to yourself. That is the wrong choice every time.

We want you to know that you have a choice. We want you to meditate because it is in those moments when the mind is quiet or partially quiet or almost quiet or quiet for a small amount of time. We laugh here because we will take what we can get! During those quiet or quiet-ish moments we capture the inner-mind's attention and tell it who we are and show it a feeling that it will remember.

When you are quiet in the mind as a practice, the mind catches on. It becomes quieted, it becomes nice, it becomes gentle, it becomes happy, it becomes carefree. It becomes less aggravated, less emotional, more balanced—and that

Chapter 5 ~ Refinement

is just the beginning, or should be.

The world's population is beginning to learn about meditation. You are teaching each other good things. Some of the things that you are teaching is that meditation will alter your emotions. It will. But it is not meditation, per se. It is us. We want you to understand this. Meditation is the method. Meditation is the classroom. It is not the lesson nor the lesson-giver.

The lesson occurs in vibrational tones that you cannot hear yet the mind can. We speak to the mind. Otherwise, we would be using a different tone that manifests as a sensation, an aroma, or an idea. When we are teaching emotional balance—and we are the Teachers of it every single time—no matter what practice you do, no matter what ritual you do, no matter what self-care you do, no matter what mindfulness technique you do or when you are doing it—your Guide and other Helpers-in-spirit are coming together to quickly give the mind a vibrational, non-verbal lesson. Guidance, if you will, on how to handle emotions differently.

After a while, you start to be love. You look around the world and you are just so loving, to the point where you are love. We explain this Teacher-student relationship in detail because not enough of you understand that we are the Teachers. We are. Your inner-mind is the student. Give us a moment with the mind and we will heal it. When it is healed, your life will be better for it.

Co-create is what we say often. Co-create with us. We will do anything that you come up with, anything that you have for us to do, anything that you are wanting to experience in this life. We help you if it is good. If it is not good we bring you another idea, a different conversation, an alternate idea to help dissuade you from going down the path that is not healthy.

We do know what is healthy and what is not. We not only see the world, but we see the patterns of the world. It is a tapestry. It is a pattern you begin to weave way over on the left, and three decades later, you are all the way on the right and you look back and you see the intricate web of threads that have formed together to create an image.

If you only planned your life the way you plan the tapestry. You would slow down, you would think first, you would not let anyone jump in the middle and mess up your threads. You would keep track of where you are. You would pace yourself and you would appreciate your accomplishment. But you would have designed it before you started. That, my friends, is the idea stage, the beginning, step one.

You started this life as an idea and then you became a child and then you grew up and then you found preference. Then you either started with mindfulness and moved about your life or you started with action and moved about your life. We want you to incorporate both. Being able to hear us is essential, from our perspective. We want it to be essential from yours.

End chapter.

CHAPTER 6

Multiplier Effect

We see you.
We see the patterns that you have created.
We see where those patterns are leading you.
Let us guide you away from it
or towards more of it.

Chapter 6 ~ Multiplier Effect

Session: 7, video: #0683
November 15, 2021

Personal Conveyance to Carol: You found the perfect spot. It is quiet. It is green. It has a backrest. It is in a corner and everything around you is alive. Plants are here and so are you, and you have been picturing doing a session here. Always do what is in your mind first and then let another idea come. It will help you out. Alright. Book-writing. Chapter Six.

Sometimes people think and then they find themselves wondering why they had the thought. We tell you that you create your own reality, because you do. Every thought that you have had you have received from the world innumerable times. We also tell you that you have intuition, and intuition is not a thought. It is guidance. We want you to understand the difference.

A thought is energy from the world. Guidance—or idea!—is from the nonphysical dimension. Why do we make such bold statements? Because we want the mind to hear us in a different way. We want it to understand that there are two places to get information. We want the mind—the inner-mind—to know that of the two, guidance is preferred. The mind knows what prefer means: better choice. Guidance is preferred.

You do not always believe that you are receiving guidance. You get an idea, you dismiss it. You think of someone, you dismiss it. You feel good about something, you dismiss it.

We want you to not dismiss guidance.

How do you know the difference between guidance and a thought? You do not. You get to decide to believe and get more or to not believe and halt your progress toward it or toward more. However, guidance is never mean, it is never nitpicking, it is never harsh or critical. It is something to do, something to look at, a solution that had not occurred to you and, yes, a solution can be substituted for guidance. That should give you a hint on which decision to make.

We offer you solutions for things that you are wanting. We see you. We see the patterns that you have created. We see where those patterns are leading you. Let us guide you away from it or towards more of it. They are not all leading you in a bad direction. Some of them are leading you very near what you have asked for: a new job, a new best friend, extra cash, something to do on the weekend. You ask for things in many ways.

Received solutions: good words for you to hear, good words for you to say. When you have those moments of clarity, pat yourself on the back and then you get more of it. You are teaching your inner-mind to lean on us when you do. It gives you what you are focused on. It gives you what you prefer. But you do not know how to identify what you prefer so you just focus, ruminate, stay angry.

The mind does not know right from wrong. It just knows what you are focused on. It has one track and if you were on a happy track, it brings you more happy. If you are on an unhappy track, it brings you unhappy. That is all.

When you receive a solution to a problem or a desire for something that you are wanting, look up and say, "Thank you, I appreciate you, let me see where this goes."

The mind understands that you are talking to God when you look up because you have been taught to look to God for

Chapter 6 ~ Multiplier Effect

answers. It matters not if you believe in God, per se—and truly it is your Guide. It matters not if you feel awkward as an adult still believing in God, thanking God, being a prayerful person. You were once a child who was taught that God loves you, that God answers your prayers and that is why I say God here. Look up when you say, "Thank you, I appreciate you. Let's see where this goes" and the mind will understand that you are not talking to it, that you are talking to your Guide.

It knows the vibrational tone that we send. We like the word God, but you misuse it. If you are reverent about God, the mind understands and adds appreciation to yours. But you are also fearful of God and so it adds fear to yours as well. Remember, now everything is based on draw. You draw things to you.

When you remain focused on something, you are drawing more like it to you. No matter what the subject, in that moment you are drawing more to you. You might receive it in that moment, or you might receive it further down the road. It matters not; it is on its way. Everything occurs because of draw.

What do you want to draw to you? We want you to draw Love, meaning us because we provide solutions to everything that you have asked for. How do you draw us? Believe in us. Accept us in your life. Offer appreciation when you receive guidance.

Your minds are beautiful. Your minds are easy for us to identify. Easy for us to look at who you are, what you are wanting and what the thought patterns of the past have been, how they have accumulated, and what you are currently manifesting.

It is easy for us to do that. It is not easy for you to do that. You make assumptions. You play with ideas. You hope that you are getting closer to the goal, whatever your goal may be. But you do not know. We do because we see the threads of thought. We see what is predominant. We see your thought patterns in the now and all of your previous nows, and we see what the mind is doing with them, which ones it has identified, categorized, labeled, and isolated as "a lot." Those are the things that are on its way.

We also know timing. Your mind cannot do what we do. Your mind pulls things toward it, things of the same likeness. Vibration is in all things. It locates similar vibration and brings it to you—the subject matters not. That is how it creates your life. What you look upon, what you feel, who you meet, where you go, what you wear, how you touch your face, or not—it is created by the mind.

It is fascinating when you think about it. What are you wanting to create? Not just what are you wanting to experience, but what are you wanting to create?

What is the difference? One puts you in the driver's seat. One does not. Your mind understands language. Words matter greatly. When you choose words, they are not random. When you choose words deliberately, you are on the path of deliberate creating. You have the capacity to alter your thinking and, because of it, alter what you experience.

You can decide how to have the things that you are wanting. You can make it easy or you can make it difficult. How do you make it easy? Decide ahead of time that the timing does not matter, but that you want it to be easy. Then

Chapter 6 ~ Multiplier Effect

say those words to yourself, "I have this thing, and it came to me easily." I have this thing AND it came to me easily again and again and again and again. It is way of tricking the mind so that it brings something to you faster. You deliberately add quantity because you keep saying you have it, then it must reply with, "I better hurry up and get it. My person thinks it is already here." If you say I usually have it, I sometimes have it—it is good, but not best. You simply have chosen to not receive quantity in the fullest amount. Do not do that!

It has to create your experience to match your words. Whether or not you have something in the present makes no difference at all. Keep saying, "I have it and it came easily." Add a smile, add a flicker of happy and then move on. A little goes a long way. A little goes a very long way. Repetition does as well. The subject does not matter. Your station in life does not matter. Everything that you have is alterable by way of words.

If you look around your life and identify things that you are wanting more of then add the word "more"—"I have so much of this, and it came easily to me. I have so much more than I used to have, and it came easily to me." Add the MORE, create the AND, and you will see extra coming into your experience.

Desire is good, desire is fun. Be playful with this; it is not meant to be a chore. It is active living and how you create your life on purpose. It is also how you create, period. Thoughts. You just did not know it.

Be careful what you watch on television. Be careful what you listen to. Be careful what you engage in. Be careful what you take in. Because that is what the mind is taking in. Quantity! What you look at and listen to over time creates your life. Everything. Nothing is excluded. And, over time, you can, by way of paying attention to what you are paying attention to, re-create what you have.

In essence, what you are doing is you are retraining the mind to receive from us, rather than pulling from the world at large. We give guidance specific for you and what you are asking for. We do not give randomly, so get that out of your mind.

If you want to be happier, we give you an idea that we know will create more joy in you. If you dismiss it, you have missed an opportunity. We do not toss out ideas. We bring ideas to the mind in a way that is different from the world at large. We give you ideas that will be—will be—easy for you. It does not know the difference in the beginning. That is where your words are important.

Go to door number one, not door number two, door number one, door number one, door number one, I like door number one, go to door number one, not two. I like door number one. I like door number one. The mind learns what you are meaning: to draw from us. We are door number one. It begins to draw from us automatically over time, and then amazing things happen. Synchronicity is everywhere: the best deals and sales, the best conversations, the best seats in the house are available when you are wanting to go, friendly faces, happy conversations in earshot, or with you.

Happy is happy, and when you notice happy it has a crystalline effect. A multiplier—and who doesn't want that? The multiplier effect—that is us in your lives when you

Chapter 6 ~ Multiplier Effect

allow us to be. What do you want multiplied? That is what this book is about, teaching your mind to locate us, prefer us, and draw from us.

End chapter.

CHAPTER 7

Partner Up

*When you have a thought, we know it.
When you have a thought, we hear it.
When you have a thought, we respond
because every thought that you have ever thought
is an asking.*

Chapter 7 ~ Partner Up

Session: 8, video: #0684
November 15, 2021

For the most part, you have no idea how often we speak to you. You have not been taught to see the signs from a young age and so you ignore them. You believe that you need to pray and hope that some kind of divine intervention will come. You do that when you are desperate for something to happen or not happen. We want you all to know we are here. We are here. Our attention is on you and we are talking to you. You do hear us, but it is only in small amounts and inaccurately for most of your lives.

If you want more signs, ask for them—and remember that you asked for them! Then look for them because you will begin see them.

There is no time commitment involved. It is easy for us to show you that we are here. Simply move about and ask for us to show you something. If you like, you might call it a test—we say "testament."

Choose something simple and watch us bring it to you. What things? Anything. Dollar bills. We will bring you signs of money. It might be opulence for you to observe—you might notice the ring on someone's hand, the car they are driving, because dollar bills are available to you. But keep your eye on the asking and then we will be able to bring dollar bills to your experience and then dollar bills for you to keep or spend as you see fit. It is all in the asking, the allowing, and then the receiving of it.

If you choose something difficult then it will be more difficult because your thought pattern on the object says it all.

If you say, "There's no way that you can bring me money or show me money," you have made it difficult for yourself to see it. Key point here. Dogear this page; highlight it as well. You SEE what your mind ALLOWS you to see. If your words include "difficult" then it will manifest difficultly seeing what you are wanting. Simple as that.

When you figure that out, you will understand that you are involved. What you think about, what you say, matters. If you choose something that you see everywhere, we will show you more of it. However, you might not register the more and say instead that you already saw it everywhere and it is not us.

We want you to choose something not extremely easy nor extremely difficult, for those are the two ends of the spectrum that will not help you believe that we are here. We are aware of you. We are aware of your question. We are aware of your desire. We are here.

Here are some examples: I want to see more numbers; I want to see more 1-2-3. I want to see more 9-4-2.

Now, as you read those numbers what was your feeling with 1-2-3? Did that feel easy or hard? 9-4-2? Did that feel easy or hard? Your feeling about the object is understood by the inner-mind. It adds your emotion of it to the asking—"Show me 1-2-3 but make it hard for me to see it. Show me 9-4-2, but make it hard for me to see it."

Here we come upon where most of your learning on the law of attraction has stopped. "Show me 1-2-3," and you are unsure if we can. That registers as, "Make it difficult." We are not teaching you how to ask us a question, for we hear your desire before you have spoken it. You might as well cancel your asking because you have had too many thoughts of the opposite.

Show me / Do not show me. The emotion is a thought. Side-by-side equals difficult. Not impossible, but difficult. You are students, we are the Teachers. We are guiding you on how to receive by way of asking.

"Show me 1-2-3, I love that number"; "Show me 9-4-2, I love that number." You change the emotion together—almost because your words have changed enough, doubled down, so to speak. But it is a good place to start.

If there is some negative emotion behind the words, some underlying background noise, it can be overcome. When you add negative emotion, "Yeah, right. Show me 1-2-3, if you can. Show me 9-4-2, if you're real," it is almost impossible...almost. Very difficult anyway because you have closed yourself down from receiving.

1-2-3, 9-4-2, or whatever your object is, it is simply a thing. We want you to have all things that you are wanting. What are you wanting?

Freedom. That about sums it up.

Freedom from getting picked on. Freedom from not enough. Fill in the blank on that one. Freedom. That is what you are wanting, freedom. Freedom to choose. Freedom to have. Freedom to go. Freedom to buy. Freedom to love upon. Freedom to be happy. Freedom to have things. Freedom to experience life or the world. Freedom to do what you want to do or what other people are able to do.

Freedom.

When you have a thought, we know it. When you have a thought, we hear it. When you have a thought, we respond,

Mind Body Connection

because every thought that you have ever thought is an asking. Every thought is a question. "I am hungry" is heard as, "I would like something to eat." "I am hungry" with a grimace, is heard as, "I would like something different or pleasing to eat." "I am sick of this," is heard as, "Heal me from boredom, remove my anger or frustration, and bring fun into my life."

We see you, we hear you, and we do not hear simple questions or simple statements. We know you, and because we know you, we know everything you are asking for with each statement, even though you do not. If you thought about it long enough you would understand what you are asking for, but we do not want you to do that. When you do, you are investigating why you are grimacing. Every moment you spend on that activity, you are creating more thoughts like it. You are amplifying the grimace.

We do not want you to be heads down, figuring things out in frustration. We want you to come upon no problems, but we know you will. When you do, we want you to breathe easy and look up, smile, and say, "This one's for you" or, "Let's partner on this one." I need you, in other words. Remain still, unthinking, and let the solution or a step towards it rise up into your awareness. If you are ready for that stage.

How do you become ready for that stage (meaning receiving from us the solution in the here and now when you have need of it)? Strong awareness of us, strong belief in us, strong love and partnering with us, and the ability for the inner-mind to look to us when you do. That is the key. Many of you try to be advanced receivers long before you are ready for it. It is not healthy on many fronts. You create

Chapter 7 ~ Partner Up

stress—unhealthy. You get angry—unhealthy. You lose faith in hearing us—extremely unwise.

How do you progress to advanced? You must begin where you are, wherever that is, each and every day. Some days you wake up on the wrong side of the bed and you begin at the beginning. Other days you wake up, you yawn and stretch, and you have joy within and you begin further ahead. How much further depends on who you are and how much you have practiced. Why, who you are? Because some of you have different areas within the Root chakra that are cleaner than others.

Why do some people get things when you do not? Many reasons, but specifically, thought patterns, emotional as well as verbal, on the topic. How often? Always. Whenever you think of the topic you add emotion. Are you steady in your desire and happiness in the having of it? Is there joyful expectation? Even in those statements there may be differences. When you add your thought plus emotion on a question alongside your beliefs about it, you come upon slowness to varying degrees.

You do not know what beliefs you have that are harmful to you. We do. We see them clearly. You may decide that you want something and you may be happy. You may like the idea of it. You may do all the joyful expectation work, yet not receive it. "Many people fall down" is a statement. What do you think about it? Did it register as true? Did it register as strange? Did it register as not true? Your answer shines a light on your belief about people falling down. Your answer might change from day to day. We do not want you to investigate your belief. We do not want you to use this exercise often on many things. You will amplify, multiply the belief. That is unwanted for you.

If you are wanting to partner with your Guide and trust them, you can learn to trust them by asking for something that is not too easy and not too difficult. You are learning to build trust in a way that makes sense. Here is the part that most of you miss: we always provide the solution—we *always* provide the solution. I like that word, solution. It is less misunderstood. I prefer solution because I want you to know we give you the answer that you are seeking, every time, without fail.

We give you the answer when you are afraid; you hold yourself apart from receiving it energetically. Many of you will say, "No, I am not. I'm open to it, I want it. I have great plans for it. I do want it. That's not true"—because you do not know what you do not know. Your beliefs play a part. Sometimes they play a major part. You can want something and have a good thought pattern, good energy on it, but you are up against a block, a bodyguard, an offensive line, and it will not allow you to have what you are asking for.

Who or what is that offensive line? Your own stored energy on the topic—and it is topic by topic, by topic, by topic. When you combine topics, you bring forward each offensive line or bodyguard or block. We want you to have everything that you are wanting. We teach you more about how to get it. We want to undo your blocks and remove that offensive line that is destructive to what you are wanting.

Thoughts matter. Emotion is a thought, so it also matters. The pattern that you have set for yourself on both are the pattern that is the block or the bodyguard or the offensive

Chapter 7 ~ Partner Up

line.

How do you get rid of it? Change your feelings about it. It is easier than you think. Change your words. Change your emotion. Change your expectation. Rephrase your asking—time and time again. Make a habit of it. It will be the best habit you have ever created, as well as the most useful.

"Show me 1-2-3" might be rephrased as, "I see 1-2-3 everywhere," as the asking. Understand this: "I see 1-2-3 everywhere" in the moment that you decide that you want it, has no negative emotional bond with the asking. There is no doubt, in other words, if you ask it this way from the start. Do this often and your lives will manifest quicker and for the better. Your mind gives you your expectation based on the words you choose. Substitute emotion for expectation. Happy thought, poor expectation equals delay. That delay can be great or small, depending on the accumulation of similar thoughts on the topic.

Make your asking specific and in a way that says you already have it. Then add this twist: say it out loud, happily. The inner-mind learns from you better out loud. When you ask silently—think them, in other words—the mind may misunderstand and assume that you are simply reading or simply thinking. Accumulation of positive pattern is less than if you ask out loud. You talk out loud, you convince out loud, you negotiate out loud, you explain things out loud, you express your enjoyment or your pleasure or your love for something out loud.

When you speak your question out loud in a way that says you have it and that you are already happy, it can assume that you believe you already have it. Then it must catch up and provide that thing that you are saying, you have. Not because that is its job but because you have said you have it. You must convince your inner-mind that you have it and then it must comply. It will seek everywhere within the world to bring it to you.

We advance your learning yet again. When you ask for simple things and you look up and you say thank you to God or to us (no matter the name, just make it the name that you are consistent with) and say simple things like "You always provide everything, everything I am wanting comes from you. I love you so much. Everything I am wanting comes from you. You always give me everything I am wanting," the inner-mind, because of repetition, because of quantity, begins to look to us specifically because you have taught it to—and we are your multiplier.

The rules for manifesting are simpler than you believe. Let these words be understood by you and then believe them so it is simpler for you. Manifesting is a subject plus timing—having something, a little or a lot, now or later, learning something new or different, remembering things. Start small, allow the mind time to learn who we are. We are the multiplier effect. Too many of you start with difficult topics or topics that you have strong doubt on. You start there because you want it or want your situation to change—we know this. But start simply and allow us to train the mind who to listen to.

Healing your body, for example, is difficult. Do not start there, do not put these words to the test to heal your body. The body is no different than any other asking, but if there is something unwell in your body, it has already accumulated to

Chapter 7 ~ Partner Up

a strong degree. In essence, you are asking to de-manifest—removal of something that you created. To de-manifest there are more layers to your asking. It is better to focus on joy than physical healing—modern term: de-stress. Remove stress from your life and your body will learn to heal. In later stages of your development, apply law of attraction techniques to your body or on your body as preventative, rather than corrective.

However, there are no limits is what I always say. Get creative—I say that too. So, yes, there are ways to heal the body. It is always best to heal the mind and the emotions along with it. This book leads to that topic.

Heal your mind, heal your emotions, and then learn the concepts; understand that thoughts create your reality. Every thought that you have ever thought remains. You are not doomed to failure because patterns can be undone, new patterns created. Ask for our help. Acknowledge our help and you will do much with your lives in ways that you are asking for.

You get what you think about. What will you think about? If this material seems too good to be true, read it again. If it seems intriguing, turn the page.

End chapter.

CHAPTER 8

Unravelling

*The mind is not trained, it just does a job
that it assumed was the right job for it.
No one trained it. No one taught it.
No one gave it a book of instructions.
It just does what it thinks it has always done.*

Chapter 8 ~ Unravelling

Session: 9 and 10, video: #0689 and 0690
November 15, 2021

Most of you have an idea of what law of attraction is. You get what you think about. Law of creating, same thing. Design your life on purpose, same thing. Mind over matter, same thing. When we teach you, we teach you what you need to know. When people teach you, they teach you what they think you should know or what they have learned or what worked for them—and always with assumption that their way is the right way for you. It is okay, truly it is, because we want you to gather information, feel good about it, and then share it. We just do not want you to share things that are unhealthy and harmful.

We describe what is healthy. Do not read between the lines and alter what we are saying. We are not going to mix words and give you insignificant information. We give you structured guidance.

When you are wanting to create something, whether or not you are aware of it, your thought pattern, your emotional pattern has gotten you where you currently are. If you like it, do more of it. If you do not like it, do the opposite. However, if you do not know what the opposite is then you are in a quandary, so do something that feels better.

Some of you are very logical, very rigid, and you want things mapped out. You want an emotional wheel so that you can look and see the opposite. We help you here to create one for yourself, because words have multiple meanings. Synonyms, antonyms—the variations are almost endless, as is your attachment and personal association with them.

On a sheet of paper, draw 20, 30, 40 segments of a wheel. Use half of it for words that you use often. Look those words up and find the antonyms. There will be many—identify one for each segment that feels like the right one for you and write it in the opposite segment.

Find another piece of paper, divide it into the same number of segments, and do it again. Only this time, identify a synonym that feels good to you.

Get another piece of paper, same number of segments, same wheel and do it again. Only this time, choose a synonym that you do not use often.

Let these be your guide for what words to choose in your patterns of speech. Your intelligence, your vocabulary, your grade level, your approach to life, your friends and family, the way you speak, is unique to you. We guide you to find the opposite, to find something similar. Then find something similar that is varied. Using these words rather than your usual speech patterns will create less quantity for the inner-mind to use.

This is why. It makes the mind pay attention to something new. Believe it or not, it will question whether or not to add quantity based on the word that you choose. "I hate that thing"; "Your breath smells terrible." Alright, let's use those two. "That is far from pleasing" and "The aroma of your breath it does not please me."

The meaning is the same, the approach is different. Awkward, perhaps, but better for you. Not only for you, but better for your relationships. There might be times when you want to let a friend know that they have something in their teeth. Non-verbal is always good. Incorporate non-verbal

Chapter 8 ~ Unravelling

when you can. The mind raises an eyebrow, so to speak, on whether or not to add quantity if words are not spoken aloud.

We go back to the previous chapter, when you are wanting to ask for help and do it out loud, look up, and thank us for helping you. Read your statement of what you are wanting out loud. Your inner-mind (substitute ego mind or subconscious mind) listens to what is heard. It understands clearly that you are saying you want something. When you read it, the mind questions whether you want it, or whether you are reading about someone wanting it, because you all read books, essays, magazine articles. Many times, they are written in the first person.

Your mind is not a know-it-all. It simply is superb in collecting, categorizing, labeling, and adding a quantity. When you use a different type of phrase than you usually do or use a different word than you usually do, the mind collects, categorizes, thinks about whether it categorized correctly; it is unsure about the label and then does not know whether to add a quantity. When you move off the subject, it does too. It skips a beat, so to speak, and no quantity is added.

Do you need to do this forever? It does not hurt. It is fun to play with language. You do not have to be fancy in your new vocabulary, just something different. The unconscious patterns life has created will pause and then unravel. That is what we mean by retrain the untrained mind. The mind is not trained, it just does a job that it assumed was the right job for it. No one trained it. No one taught it. No one gave it a book of instructions. It just does what it thinks it has always done.

There are histories upon histories, upon histories,

evolutions of man upon evolutions of man. Eventually, the mind gets curious on what it is supposed to do. In the beginning—histories ago, evolutions of man ago—it put a kink in the works, it was shaken up, put a cog in the wheel. You get the idea. It made a U-turn that it was not prepared for and is scrambling to catch up. That is good. That means it is on an upward learning track.

If you are going down a track of indecision (meaning the inner-mind has started to manifest you as indecisive), you do not want that. It can wreak havoc with your life in so many ways. If you find yourself becoming less interested in selecting an option, this is you as indecisive. I hope you noticed the wording of that phrase. I did not say, "Should you notice not being able to make up your mind," which adds definitiveness to the statement. Retrain the mind by intentionally choosing to speak differently.

It is not about intelligence; it is about purposeful speaking. Can you overdo it? No. Can you underdo it? Yes, of course. You have been. You have been talking and using ghastly phrases your entire life. Your life, whatever it has in it, is an accumulation of the way you have chosen to speak, as well as what you have chosen to listen to. Teach your mind something new. Choose your words carefully. Phrase them in a way that still conveys meaning.

Many times, you respond to a situation with a lot of words and most of those words are unhelpful. Sometimes it is meaningless speaking to be heard, force your opinion, challenge others just because you did not like them—not necessarily because you value your opinion more and feel the need to express it. Some of you just argue for the sake

Chapter 8 ~ Unravelling

of arguing, along with many other things. Choose what to respond to, as well as how to respond: a shrug, a noise that means "maybe"; a tilt of the head that says "maybe not"; a nod that means, "I might." They are used less often and so they are still good—and better than your usual phrases such as, "Oh, I don't know" or "I think I might."

Let's take "I think I might" as the next example. "I think I might"—there is indecision all over that one. Unsure, questionable, non-authoritative equals a toss-up on whether or not you will like the outcome. You are putting it out there, you are training the mind with your word choices, and these say, "Please give me an outcome that is questionable." Phrased another way, "Bring me whatever the heck you feel like, I will deal with it later."

The better thing to say is, "I have an easy time making decisions and life always works out for me. I have a knack for picking the best on every subject. Life is easy for me. I have an easy time. I love life." Some of those will be hard for you to say and mean it. Pretend that you were speaking to someone, it will be easier. Add your half of the conversation only and it gets easier still. Much easier with practice.

Let's say that you want to buy a new car. You have the money and you are undecided on whether or not to get one. How would you handle that situation? Normally, you would simply tell people, "I don't know, I am thinking about getting a new car. It's not the money. I just don't know what I want." That approach to speaking is riddled with "I don't know."

What should you say instead? Number one, you could choose not to say anything until you have decided and that is the best choice, but you still have self-talk to master.

Does that matter? Yes, it does. It is fifty percent! That does make a difference. You might try something like this, "I love looking at new cars. I like big ones, I like small ones. I like four-doors and two-doors and I like hatchbacks. I like new cars." Then you might advance it to, "It was easy picking out my new car. I knew the minute I saw it that it was the one for me. I love it. It has everything I want."

You could advance it still and add details. "I feel good in it. I like the price, I like the color. I like the seats. I like how comfortable it is. I like the stereo. I like the interior. I like how it drives. I like the sound it makes when I start it up. I like everything about it. I love my car. I loved buying it. I loved looking for it. I love driving it home. I love how easy it was to select it. I love how easy it was for it to become mine. I love how I felt the whole time that I was looking and purchasing my new car. I love how I felt the whole time."

That has interest and ease all throughout. What does that do for you? Everything. Your words are what create your life. The very first time you use this technique, will it work perfectly? I want you to say yes, of course it will—even though it might not. Your mind is making a U-turn and is not necessarily all the way around the bend, not necessarily picking up speed and going the other direction—yet! Don't care. Keep doing it. You have years of life, years of quantities, years of patterns that are now built into your lives.

You are making a difference in your life when you do this technique and that difference can happen quickly. So add this in to help yourself, "I started practicing retraining my mind and changes came quickly for me. Everything I have is because I retrained my mind quickly. My mind responded

Chapter 8 ~ Unravelling

quickly. I love rephrasing things, it was easy for me to do. I followed the examples and it just became fun and easy. I do it all the time and my life is just amazing. It just came easy. Everything comes easy for me. I love that life is good, life is easy, life is fun. I love my life." And then stop there.

When your mind starts going down a track of "This is not real, this is not good for me," you have gone a little too far. Back it up a little bit. Find a phrase that feels good. Get yourself back on the right track—and then wrap it up. It is meaningful to end with, "I love my life" and saying it in a way that is playful yet sounds real to you. If you say it bland, "I love my life, I love my life," you get one point. If you say, "I love my life," with a downward glance, you get no points. You do not go backward, you just do not get advancement. Add inflection, add positive tone. "I love my life!" Make it powerful. "I love my life! Love my life!" You get two points. It is the words plus emotion, that is what I am getting at.

Words plus positive emotion gets you there faster. I like to say, "You get what you think about." Thoughts create things. When it comes down to it, you simply did not learn this early enough in life to have already made a habit of it. Start now. You start new habits all the time. You buy a new home, you put your dishes in a new cabinet. You get a new job which causes you drive a different direction to work. It is a new habit and new habits are fun.

"Everything is always working out for me"; "I love my life"; "Life is easy"; "I never argue"; "I never have a hard time."

"I always have a great time." is even better.

"I always have a great time"; "I never have a hard time"—read these two aloud and feel what it does in your belly. There is a vibration, a rumble, a feeling of dissatisfaction. A feeling of not as good as the other one, because it is not, but it is better than the alternative, which is that "life sucks." So many of you say life sucks in a lot of different languages, in a lot of different ways, with a lot of different tones beneath it.

Do this often on every subject, including the subject of being able to use this technique. It is not hard work. It does not need to take over your life either. If you start getting frustrated, you are applying it too often or on too many things. Just back up a little. Do not give up—that is the wrong answer. Just back up a little. When you do, you, and your beliefs, and the inner-mind, all feel better. And when you feel better, we get to bring you more solutions.

End chapter.

CHAPTER 9

Inter-Mind Communication

*When the mind starts to prefer our tone,
it loses sight of anger and frustration.
When it loses sight of anger and frustration,
you stop noticing the occurrence of them.
You become gentler by nature.
You are the echo of the inner-mind.*

Chapter 9 ~ Inter-Mind Communication

Session: 11, video: #0691
November 15, 2021

Personal Conveyance: Today is November 15, 2021 and it is 11:00 o'clock in the morning, or thereabout. We are happy and healthy this morning. We always are, Carol, you are as well. Good job. The note on the door is perfect. Let's do that every time because they do come in and out of the room. I like that you wrote, No service please, I am tidying up—that was me suggesting it to you. You like to be friendly. "Do not disturb" and "Please do not disturb" were both still too rough, I am glad you thought about it longer. Tidying up is nicer.

NOTE: We are still on the cruise and Carol had a worry line about her cabin steward interrupting the dictation video to take care of her room. The worry was strong enough that I decided to address it verbally. Before the cruise she and I talked about book-writing and which ones could be completed. She was/is eager to have us write her memoir of her awakening. She plans for it to be a book as well as a movie. Very detailed she is; we have convinced her to focus on this book and stay with the Plan we have for her.

Mind Body Connection is the book that needs to be completed. We're not going to forget Dots Connected but I love that you are dedicated to this book, you understand why. And yes, you can come back on this cruise and write the other book if we don't get to it. I do have another book after this one planned and if you don't mind, I would like to do that while on this cruise. The story of how you came to be who you are is a story that will be written. But if we can get these books done, Carol, then you've got something that you can use. The third book—well, there are many—but the third book is needed; we have a plan for it. Ocularity of the Mind, book one; Mind Body Connection, book two; Manifestation of the True Self, book three. We begin dictation for Chapter Eight.

When you begin to speak for us that means that you enjoy the topic of Source. When you begin to speak for us that means you are recognizing that you have many things to say in support of us. That is when you, the human being speaks for us.

When you receive from us, you then speak the words that were received—or so you think. That is the difficulty that so many of you have. You doubt or you do not doubt enough. In either event you are attracting more of whatever you have. Let me explain.

If you are working on your ability to communicate with us and you love it, you are receiving, hearing voices, sentences are given to you. You might see words, you might see pictures. It is the voices, generally, that you believe.

On the one hand, I want you to believe that the words you are receiving are correct because if you add doubt then the mind adds more doubt. The mind is already adding in the beginning (contaminating). It cannot not do it but it is like asking the mind to mess you up further when you add your doubt. You say things such as, "Well, I don't know, I think I might have heard somebody say, "Cash it in" but it was really quiet, so I don't know."

That sentence is not serving you. Simply say, "I heard or I received, 'Cash it in.'" It was a voice and it was softly given."

Chapter 9 ~ Inter-Mind Communication

You could say softly received, but then you put the problem on yourself. Softly given simply makes a statement that whoever gave you the information sent it softly, therefore it was received correctly—tips and tricks are what this is! There is confidence in the latter. Always speak with confidence.

Here is the "yeah, but": in the beginning, the mind is wrong. Generally, it is giving you a word or phrase or sentence that feels loving because the vibrational tone that we are sending is purity of love. It will not add aggravation or a statement of criticism of any kind; it cannot. Those two things do not go together—feeling our love and aggravation. Soft, loving vibrational tone means that your mind will give you a soft and loving phrase.

The words will be whatever the mind wanted to give you based on how you are feeling. If you have been thinking about the world at large, the mind might say, "The world is a beautiful place. Smile more and be happy, because we love you." If you have been thinking about your work, the mind might say, "Love everything that you do and be happy, because we love you."

The mind will give you what it does because it feels swooning. It feels enraptured with the frequency we send to it. Then it gives you words based on what you have been thinking about, perhaps what you might be considering doing and you receive a quote unquote "message" from your Guide.

We love all messages that the mind creates, and in the beginning it does—but a loving statement is a loving statement, and so there is no harm. But understand if the mind produces something for you on command with no specific instructions, we will say, "Well done." We want you to understand we are asking the mind to produce words, always words. Pictures, sensations they are nice to have, but they do not convey enough meaning.

When the mind becomes tired we move to another ability, a sensation, an aroma, a word or two. Rest. An idea, a picture, a word or two. Rest. You get the idea. We allow the mind to give you whatever it wants to give you in the beginning. If it is very stubborn, it does not produce anything for you. Do not let that bother you. Come back again and again and again and again.

It is good for you to have a rhythm or a pattern in your practice sessions so that the mind understands that you are ready to receive from your Guide. However, do not be so rigid that you are not able to teach the mind that you are wanting to receive anywhere and everywhere, to be able to do nothing or a lot of something and receive. Regular pattern equals training, irregular pattern equals training. You get to choose your training. There are some methods that are better than others and there are specific methods that are the best.

Which one do you want? The best answer is a question—which one is the best for my mind? If we have private instruction or consultations with you, we will give you specific information. But for most of you, we want you to vary it up. Have a place and time that you receive. Early in the morning is very good, the mind has less things that it is thinking about. Make it easy on yourself. If you wait until later in the day, simply relax your mind for a minute or two first. There is no need to hurry.

There is also no need to wait. All of you, no matter your age or background or education or even your own interest

Chapter 9 ~ Inter-Mind Communication

in it, is ready for us to get to work on teaching your inner-mind how to look for us, identify us, locate us, receive from us, translate, and then produce. It is always in that order.

You have five hundred straws in front of you. All of them are striped with a color. One of them is stripe-less. The mind scans and sees straw, straw, straw, straw, straw, straw, straw, white. Then pauses because of it. Scan, scan, scan, scan, straw, straw, straw, straw, straw, straw, straw, straw, straw, white. Pause again. Back to scanning. It sees the different color stripes, and it knows them as vibration—angry, happy, sad, lighthearted, curious, inquisitive, et cetera. It finds the white and it knows pureness. It simply categorizes, labels, and moves on.

It categorizes us (the white straw, I like my analogy here) as love. A different kind of love—purity. Purity. We help the mind to consistently, among all the other frequencies, find ours. It is a sightless job that the inner-mind is doing. Remember that. It is not you with eyes, it is not the you that thinks in other words. We are talking about a second nature of you and that part of you is sightless. It simply scans the environment for vibrational tones, meaning frequencies. Ours is pureness. Pure. Pure. Pure.

It is pure. It is a tone that has zero density. We are love. We are intelligence and we are speaking to you specifically. The mind enjoys the feeling of love—our kind of love. But there is so much for the mind to keep track of. It registers that we exist initially, and then gets back to work.

When you sit quietly in a no-thought kind of meditation, it is a moment that we have to draw that radar to us, very gently loop a love cord around its nose and simply draw it to us. *Come this way, come this way, come this way.* You have a thought—we let the cord go. You set the thought aside and we begin again—*Come this way, come this way, come this way.*

You will notice that your meditation becomes easier because the mind prefers our tone over everything else in the world. It is why meditation, quiet mind meditation, works on your emotions first. When the mind starts to prefer our tone, it loses sight of anger and frustration. When it loses sight of anger and frustration, you stop noticing the occurrence of them. You become gentler by nature. You are the echo of the inner-mind.

After some time, the mind knows what you are wanting it to do when you sit down at a certain time and place. It is prepared to do the thing that you have taught it. Let's say you sit down at 7:00 p.m. every day and you sit in the red chair and that is where you do your receiving work. You have your notepad, your logbook, and your pen handy and you sit and you do your breath work and then you ask to receive. If you do that pattern day after day, after day, after day, after day, the mind understands the pattern. So, when you have your logbook and your pen handy and you sit down at 7:00 p.m., it prepares to turn its radar towards us. You naturally receive cleaner than any other time during the day. Caution here—do not over-practice at any one time or place or you could teach the mind to NOT receive at any other time!

The mind is a pattern-maker. You have to do it enough times for the pattern to become understood. We encourage you to do it as a routine, as a practice. Not so rigid that you cannot receive in any other location or time, however. In

Chapter 9 ~ Inter-Mind Communication

the early stages it is good to have structure, that is all. If you receive within five minutes—good. Get up, move about, you are done.

It is not, in the beginning, the time for you to expect two-way conversation. Your inner-mind, the student within, does not yet know how to do that. It also does not yet know how to interpret what we are saying and give it to you. What it does know is that it loves the frequency of Source. It will always bring you a gentle message, but it gives you its own message first.

If you are quiet and gentle by nature, the mind might learn quickly. Might. If you have beliefs in you that receiving is wicked or evil, or if you are prone to fear, and small things scare you, quiet, by nature, might not matter. It could still be difficult for you to learn, but not impossible. Meditation and energy work will conquer these issues and then you will be able to learn faster.

We want everyone to have a quiet and supple mind. It is the best because the mind can locate us easily, even among all of the things that it has in front of it. It knows even when you are busy, even when you are thinking, even when you are running, even when you are sweating, even when you are stressed. It knows how to find us once your mind is quiet and supple.

It might not have an ability to keep track of everything that you are doing in the moments you are doing them and also receive from us, but it will know where we are. That is what we mean by quieted. It keeps an eye on us. The fewer things that you are thinking about, the fewer things that you are stressed about, less things that you are doing physically

Mind Body Connection

the more its attention can be placed on us. That is fun.

When the mind gives us attention, we teach it. We always start with how to locate us without the string from us drawing it to us. Automatic location device is what we teach first because that is the best place to start. Teaching the mind to interpret our vibrational tone and the intelligence within it is what all of you are wanting—instant gratification, instant recognition. You may want it, but we do not start there. It is not the best place for you. The mind will be more prone to error if we started with Chapter Ten instead of Chapter One.

We are teaching it a new subject, one that you have not learned. You might like the idea of it, you might enjoy the idea of it. You might have read books on it. You might have educated yourself. You might have gotten readings. You might have dabbled here and there, but you have not learned how. It is another language.

When you sit to receive, do so with the intention to hear us. Whatever you get, write it down, date it, and add some small description. "It was a voice, it was quiet, sounded like my own. It was a voice, it was booming, and was very masculine. It felt as though it was on the left-hand side and then moved to the right." That is all you need to put in your logbook.

In the beginning, how do you know when to write the message that you think you heard? You do not. How do you know when the message is less contaminated? You do not. Unless we are your Teachers, by way of a physical meeting through a channel or a clairvoyant teacher who sits—not stands—sits and receives one by one by one for the duration of the class and tells you what we are saying. That teacher

Chapter 9 ~ Inter-Mind Communication

must be qualified to hear our instruction and validation. There will always be inaccuracies through a clairvoyant medium, however.

A channeler who allows us to speak out loud through them to teach you is always best. We guide you and validate for you what you are receiving and how accurate you are. We confirm whether you have reached the lessons on becoming accurate in meditation. We convey to you what step your training is in while meditation is occurring, as well as how well your meditation is going, and so on.

You do not know if your teacher—meaning a human, straightforward teacher—has consulted with us prior to your class session. There are many titles of such classes—"Unfoldment into Mediumship"; "Intuitive Studies Class"; "Meet your Spirit Guide"; "How to Channel"—but it matters not. They rarely communicate with us prior to in preparation and, rarer still, throughout the class session to guide you properly.

There is no human being that can tell you if you are accurate. Zero. None. This woman, Carol, that I am speaking through now, she cannot on her own, but she knows it. She would not attempt to. She would say, "I have no idea if you received, but let me check. Let's find out. It sounds pretty cool what your mind gave you, what you received, let's find out how accurate it was."

But she is a channel. She receives in the mind voices, pictures, sensations—all the things that people attribute to ocular receiving. She trusts us and knows who the Teachers are. Her mind locates us instantly. Gravitates towards, allowing us to form the words on her tongue and then responds instantly when we ask the mind to go ahead and say it. She sees words, hears a phrase, and knows that if we say it (aloud), then it is said. Then it is said. Because she also is the echo of her inner-mind. Her inner-mind sits there and simply says, "Are you going to say that phrase? I'm curious." But it does not assume that it is to be said; it asks us first.

She can hear us in the mind's eye during the pauses of speaking out loud. Her mind has learned well and learned easily. She has done it many lifetimes and so that aspect of her Being comes forward. The reason for that is simple: she was pre-destined for it. It was built into this lifetime for her to have the ability to be a channel. So, yes, it did and does come easier for her and others like her.

She did not know in the beginning that it was built-in. She simply knew it happened almost overnight. She also loved it so much, she taught her mind by way of her constant attention on this ability to receive us anywhere and everywhere, running up hills included. "Let me see what I get!" she would say. She did not ask questions and expect to receive an answer of significance. She simply ran up a hill and said, "Don't lose sight of me. What are you saying? Let me hear you. It also distracts my mind, by the way, and all of a sudden, I'll be at the top of the hill. That was easy. Let's do that again."

As she was running, she would (and still does) raise a finger or blink an eye as a non-verbal method of communicating that she heard us. "I heard that. Got it. Heard it, got it." Or felt it, because some things are given as a sensation—a pat on the back, someone grabbing her hand and pulling her up

Chapter 9 ~ Inter-Mind Communication

the hill faster; she can see it. It is a perceived experience and she is very good at it.

She has practice sessions with us every single day as she is brushing her teeth. She stops and says, "This is what I heard, while brushing my teeth. Is that something I need to know? Or is it just practice?" We tell her just practice, or that we need to talk to her about whatever it was. She says okay. But if it is practice, she does not push nor say anything more about it. She smiles, looks up and to the right, and says, "Thank you, I'm really good at this. I love my practice sessions."

She loves hearing when other professionals still have practice sessions. We encourage professionals to always practice on their own or with others that match their skill level or with a teacher who is qualified—a seasoned professional. It matters not if you were taught from a straightforward teacher or if you were self-taught. Your mind is making errors unless you are a channel. How do you know if you are a channel? Because you have had the conversation and we leave it at that.

If you are someone who is not interested in having conversations with us, do not worry about it. You are simply not ready for it. But if you are reading these words then you are more ready than some. *If* is a big word. It just might define your future. You use it casually, flippantly. We use it on purpose. We do know who you are as you are reading this book. We do watch what your mind is doing as you are reading the book. You will have ocular experiences as you read the book. There is no need to consider them as gifts or messages. We are talking to the mind while it is reading the words with you. It—the sub-conscious mind—is receiving from us as your eyes are reading the page.

How many things can you do at one time? Two, eventually: whatever your physical body is doing and locating us by way of the inner-mind. In the beginning, you must be doing nothing for us to teach the mind to locate us. For that is the beginning, always.

End chapter.

CHAPTER 10

Retraining Is Necessary

*You have a built-in ability to influence
what you think about—what you receive,
what you create. You call it free will.
We say, an ability. It is an ability
automatically built-in for every single person.
Not one of you is deficient in it.*

Chapter 10 ~ Retraining Is Necessary

Session: 12, video: #0692
November 15, 2021

Who am I to be a Teacher? I am, and have been in this role for quite some time. Some of us are newer at it than others within The Jeshua Collective or within the levels of us that teach. Speaking generally here—once upon a time we became a Being in the nonphysical dimension and then we grew up. That is why we are Teachers and Healers and why we came upon the ability to teach you.

I am one among many that speak through this woman, Carol. We are the Teachers of the ones that are in charge of your life. We sometimes say we are the Teachers of Teachers (capital T on both). You have found us here in the world by way of a human being who created an opportunity to quiet her mind in such a way that the channeled ability that was built-in came to the surface. When it did, she loved it so much that it blossomed almost overnight. And here she is. Now we get to speak through her and teach you who we are, remind you that the mind has no capacity to translate vibrational communication without being taught.

There is an ability under the surface in all of you. Some of you, it is right under the surface. That is where Carol's was. For others, it is further under the surface. Why is that? Two main reasons: Birth Intention and the willingness of your physical mind.

If you have both, as Carol did, then you will require very little effort on your part to have the desire to sit quietly, meditate, and learn to receive. You will gravitate towards the desire for wanting this ability easily. It will be almost unbearable to not meditate. You will feel the need to do it, even if you are running late. You will stop and say, "No, I need to get my meditation in, it is important." It will become important. It will become a need. It will become something that you cannot not do. Not receive from us, meditate. At some point meditation will be necessary for you.

Meditation is easier for a quiet person who simply does not have an active thought process, someone who does not have consistent thoughts, has a quiet mind by nature. Those people have an advantage. Do not worry whether that is you. Do not fret, because we teach everyone. No mind is incapable of being taught.

There are small moments throughout the day where we teach you to gravitate towards the Life Path subjects that are built-in for your life experience. For ocularity and channeled abilities, meditation is a requirement because training is required to translate vibrational communication. We are teaching you in meditation to become an interpreter for us.

Built-in is what we refer to as Birth Intentions. They are life purpose types of things. You have more than one and we do help you throughout your life on them. Meditation is the very best way to receive guidance to advance yourself with them. Meditation is non-verbal, always. We are speaking to the inner-mind every single time. It is first stage learning. Second stage are the things that you do because of it. It learns first, then gives it to you.

Remember now, your Higher Being created or built-into your life these Birth Intentions, Soul Plan is another way of describing them. They are the things that you wanted to do in this lifetime before you became a person. That is how

Chapter 10 ~ Retraining Is Necessary

life works. Do not be frustrated if you are not a spontaneous channel. You might have been in another lifetime. There is joy in learning, no matter what. There are things that Carol cannot do or has not done. There are things that are challenging in life for her. It just happens to be becoming a channel was not one of them. Be happy for her. Allow her to feel good about the ease of its becoming and then remember that you too experience ease in other areas.

There are subjects that come easily to each of you. We want her to rejoice in the ease of her learning (accepting) the channeling ability and be okay with being challenged on a different subject. When you are an allower, your mind becomes softer. Appreciate what you can do, appreciate what others can do. Be an appreciator—be a lover, not a fighter. In other words, "Judge not, lest ye be judged."

What that simply means is if you are filled with envy that this ability came easy for her, then you are filled with envy and this ability will become more difficult for you. Envy will also be more pervasive in your life. You do not want that. "Judge not, lest ye be judged," is a reminder in a religious phrase that whatever you think about you get more of in your own life—and you do not want that.

"Be happy, lest you be happy" does not have the same ring to it. How about, "Be happy and get more of it?"; "Judge others and get more of it." It is the way your mind works because it is an attractor of whatever you think about. It is a two-way feed. It absorbs, gives to you. You think about what has been given to you, meaning whatever is prevalent on your mind, and then the attractor has more on that subject. It is this endless loop.

Mind Body Connection

The loop is not unteachable because you have ears and a brain and you can make choices and you can influence. That too is built-in for everyone. You have a built-in ability to influence what you think about—what you receive, what you create. You call it free will. We say, an ability. Think of it as an ability because it is. It is an ability automatically built-in for every single person. Not one of you is deficient in it.

Be very happy about that. Stop calling it free will. The term is overused and does not serve you. The ability to influence your mind is what this chapter is all about. How do you do it? The ways are almost endless. Create your reality by way of thoughts plus emotions. It is a short chapter, but we are not done with it yet. But that is the point and is, in essence, all that needs to be said. Your mind, however, needs to hear more so I say more.

Influence is all around you. Everything you look at, everything you take in, everything you hear, everything you watch, everything you engage in, everything you are aware of, and everything that you are not aware of, is influence.

What you are aware of obviously has stronger influence. You are aware of a sunset, you are aware of a thunderstorm. You are aware of dust, you are aware of dust mites at the same time. You are aware of bubbles and you are aware of bubble baths at the same time. The mind is complicated and is very much like a web or net. A single subject touches many threads.

When you see the color blue, there is a chain reaction and it knows all of the blue that you have ever seen. It knows because of the net, so to speak. It takes in your surroundings, all of it. Your present awareness does not have the capacity

Chapter 10 ~ Retraining Is Necessary

to take in—or acknowledge, better said—how much your mind absorbed.

The room that you are in at this moment in time, for instance, is being absorbed the entire time that you are in it, not just the moment you stepped into that room or environment. It is a constant reinforcement that it is receiving visually, audibly, sensory perception. As well, everything has a vibrational tone, a vibratory element within it. You are aware of the physical attributes, the noises, rough or hard or soft. You are not aware of the vibrational essence of each object, but your inner-mind is.

It is aware of your emotions as well. It is collecting and gathering, categorizing and labeling, and adding a quantity to thousands of things in each and every second. That almost sounds like your mind is not re-trainable, but yet it is.

Some things are filed way in the back. Those are the things that you did not have conscious awareness of. In plain terms, you did not notice them, your inner-mind absorbed them, had awareness of them, but you did not physically notice them. The vibrational tones that were received from things you noticed in or about the room that you were in are filed accordingly, and those are the things that have the most influence.

Take a moment, look around your room. What do your eyes land on in this moment? You are not being guided. This is not an intuition-based exercise. Simply look around your room. We have in this moment given you a clean slate. Is it hot, is it cold? Is it light, is it dark? Do you notice the cushions, do you notice the furniture, do you notice colors, do you notice patterns? Do you notice an element? What do you notice?

Now, close your eyes for about ten seconds and look around the room again. What else do you notice? A new bud on a plant? A shoe out of place, a cord dangling? The hum of the air conditioning or the whistle of the teapot? Your mind is absorbing everything in the room and identifying new things to you.

Who are you as a person? You are the echo of what you have taken in. Some of those things have become so strong that we use the word belief. A belief is something that simply has a quantity that is far greater than anything else. It is a quantity-based reality that you are living in.

Why is pink pleasing to you, but not on a car? But not on someone over the age of thirty? Because you have taken in many things of that color that were pleasing and some that were not. Everything that is not is human interference that has stopped you from enjoying that color everywhere on everything. From enjoying over-pink-ified.

You have designers who combine colors and show you that combining colors is good. They show you so many different combinations that you learn that one color is not as good unless you come upon a designer who is profitable on designing rooms or clothing selections of a single color. If others get on that bandwagon, then it becomes a trend and then you suddenly like pink everywhere because it is allowed.

Human influence is far greater and far more consistent than you realize. That might seem like an extreme example, but is it? It is not. When I say absorbs everything in your environment, I mean absorb. Takes in, but also soaks in the

Chapter 10 ~ Retraining Is Necessary

vibration of your thoughts on it. It takes in the object and your thoughts on it. It is a memory bank activity.

When you see a green rug, your inner-mind immediately thinks back on every instance that you have seen a green rug and whether it was pleasing to you. Whether others around you said it was pleasing. "Whether" each and every time because the mind takes in emotion as it is absorbing the objects; it then categorizes both simultaneously. Green and rug is good, or green and rug is bad. That is how you like green rugs or do not like green rugs.

That opinion can and does change over time based on influence at large. This is not a bad thing. It is simply influence. Influence is built-in. You get to influence your own mind. Now we get to the how—by enjoying everything around you. If you see a green rug and your initial reaction is, "I do not like that"—that is your indicator that you have been in environments where there was a green rug and you have not enjoyed the look of it, someone else did not enjoy the look of it and mentioned it, or there was an argument in the room and your eyes were fixated on the green rug while it was occurring.

There is some assemblance of memories that have been formed that has given you the opinion that you have in that moment. You are drawing to you more green rugs, things to not enjoy as well as amplifying not enjoying rugs.

If you are trying to redecorate your bedroom and you want a rug in the room, you bring that forward. You might have more difficulty in selecting a rug, especially if you have trained your mind to believe that you have difficulty picking out colors. On it goes and on it goes and on it goes. It is a web of information or a net, as I have said. It is always best to simply say, "I like this. This is always easy. My life is easy. I like this. That's nice. I enjoy it. I always know what my preferences are. It's easy for me to identify my preference. It's easy for me to identify the thing that I'm going to enjoy the most for the longest amount of time. When I decorate things, I love it forever. I always love the way I decorate. I enjoy doing it. It's always my favorite."

Play with those words. Use them often and you will retrain your mind to like more things. When you like more things, you have less aggravation in your life. Your mind settles down. The vibrational tone of discord is rough. If you are a selector—I like this, not that; I like this, I like that; I do not like this; I do not like this; I do not like this; I like that—you have a mixture of both. It is much better to say, "I like all of these things, but that one is my preference."

The emotional tone of discord is not present in that statement. "I like it, and…", is present. That creates an opportunity for your mind to have less dense vibrations running through it and that makes your mind an easier candidate to become a channel.

It also makes you a better conversationalist. More people will enjoy talking to you because you are happy. You phrase things in ways that do not bother people. "That person is always happy. I like hanging around them." You will draw more people to you that are happy. The ones who are not won't come into your experience if you are someone that is happy and also enjoys being happy and enjoys having people around you that are happy. You cannot be over-happ-ified.

If you say things like, "Everybody around me is always

Chapter 10 ~ Retraining Is Necessary

happy, I always feel good. I always feel like doing things and everybody I come in contact with is so friendly. I love that. I love my life. I love that I am an attractor of happy and of joy. Life is just so full of joy. I love my life. Now what am I going to do today?" You could sit in that joyful state and create happy, but not experience it if you do not act upon additional thoughts that come to you. I do not want you to do that. I want you to do something with that joyful, quiet mind.

There are a lot of fun things in the world to do, go out and do them. But do not overlook the opportunity to receive from us while you are out and about in the world. It is, after all, what is supposed to happen.

This ability to retrain the mind is built-in. Why? So you become happy. So you enjoy your life. Yes, all of that is true. The truest answer, though, is so you can hear us, so you guide yourself to the desire to learn to hear us verbally. Verbally is the goal.

If the ability to retrain the mind to influence your own mind was not built-in then life would be futile. You would not ever be able to hear us, your inner-mind, the sub-conscious mind would run the show—period. So it must be built-in.

The purpose of life is whatever your Higher Self built in. "Purposes of life" is a better way of phrasing it, and there are many. One that is always built-in is to gravitate towards things that are pleasing to you, no matter what they are. "Pleasing things" has a joyful connotation, not things that you do because you make a lot of money at it. You can make a lot of money and hate your job. That is not happy. Having a lot of money might bring you joy, but is negated if you do not like your job.

Many of you do not understand that if joy is truly built into the thing that you are doing then happy begets happy. Joy begets joy. Love begets love. Arguing begets arguing as well. Whatever you focus on, you get more of.

Built-in ability to be able to influence your own subconscious mind is necessary for everyone. Some of you will decide that life is a party waiting to happen and sit on the fence and watch others be happy and wait for your time to come. Others will decide that life is not a party and make do with what they have. Neither of those is joy nor happy nor loving to yourself.

I want you to understand that looking around your day, your life, your world, and finding ways to see it as pleasing is good for you. Find things that please you and do them or enjoy them, talk about them so more of your life is pleasing. That is a given. Why? Why do I say that again and again? Because when you are happy, you hear us!

It begins with intuition. When you are happy, your intuition is better. For some of you, that will be enough. If you are reading this book, then that is not enough because you would not have found it or opened it if it was. Some part of you is wanting information on ocular abilities.

This is a good subject, so allow it to take form in your life. Do the exercises and let this settle on you in a new way. You came into this life to be a person. You had some things built-in. Because of it, some things will come easily to you. Do those things and love on the fact that it came easily. Find other things that you want to do and do them. Enjoy your attention on it and be at peace with your choices.

Chapter 10 ~ Retraining Is Necessary

When something is difficult, breathe joy into it and it will become easier. Worry not if it was easy to begin with. If you only do the things that are easy that is okay, but not everything is built-in to be easy. We do not build things in to be difficult, but we do not build-in easy on every subject that you might want to experience in life.

When it comes to ocular abilities, everyone has these things: the ability to influence the mind on what it will enjoy, and the ability to hear us in non-verbal ways. That is all.

Some Soul Beings will choose to build-in more. Maybe yours did, maybe yours did not. It matters not because your mind can be taught. You are constant learners. Ocular communication with us that leads to verbal communication with us can be learned. Easy or hard has no place in the conversation at all. True, it will come easily or easier if it is built-in. It will come about eventually if it is not. The pace is not for you to set. But you can help by making time for meditation, enjoying the topic, looking forward to your practice sessions, and following the structure of the exercises.

We are not human teachers that make assumptions. What we teach and what we ask you to do is the best way for your mind to learn this new language the fastest.

End Chapter.

CHAPTER 11

Manifesting On Purpose

*The human mind receives vibrational tone
from all directions.
When you ask for something,
it (your inner-mind) places emphasis
on your desire for the inner-mind
to place its preference on us.
Then you get what you are wanting faster.*

Chapter 11 ~ Manifesting On Purpose

Session: 13 and 14, video: #0694 and 0696
November 16, 2021

Personal Conveyance: November 16, 2021. Interesting, Carol! You were about to say 2019. Would you like to know why? I want to tell you! Because you're on a cruise and the mind is looping back. Looping back, looping back to that cruise. You enjoyed it and you are enjoying this one and the reason for that particular looping—"similar" is what you heard in the mind. Lobos and Las Olas—there is some mind activity saying "same but different, same but different. Is this 2019? Source was with us then. Is this the same?" Now, it knows that we are here but it also knows that there is something different. You are on a cruise, we are here, but there is something different. And so, it just selected the date to try to force it to be the same as last time. That is just a phenomenon of your mind. How do you like that? Just a moment. We begin the next chapter now.

NOTE ADDED: Lobos was the name of the cabin steward for the November 2021 cruise. It was the same ship, Celebrity Edge, that Carol went on a few weeks into "face spelling" April 2019. She was in a daze the entire time. There was a heightened sense of all of us. Las Olas is the road that leads to the port in Fort Lauderdale. Six months earlier, it was predicted to her through a reading that Las Olas would lead to an important event. There are many details about that cruise that are undeniably Source-given and is the subject for the Dots Connected book reference. At the time of publication for this book, Dots Connected: Project Canary as the subject was extended. We will undoubtedly use Dots Connected as a chapter in different book.

Mind Body Connection

If you do not know where you are going, how do you know you will get there? I like the phrase. It is people teaching people the right thing. Design your life on purpose. I like the phrase. It is us teaching people what we want you to know.

There are things for you to read if you are wanting ocularity. Which things? Channeled works or anything that helps you become happy in general. Are you happy when you are reading them? Yes. Are you happy reading an epic novel about war and destruction? No, you are not. It is an activity that you are doing. You may think that your favorite is epic war novels or history novels. You might know a lot about the topic; it may interest you. Okay, you are having an interested moment, but you are not happy. There is no sparkle within your vibration.

There is no observation from us that you are in joy, in joy, but you are in interest. I want you to not be interested in war and death and destruction or maiming, nor any of the things that go along with it.

Just from identifying a series of items, as I just did, that are similar, each of your minds added on at least one more item to that last paragraph. That is the super-attractor within and it is a *super* attractor. It is constantly bringing things to you. What it does, it does well. But it does not do what you ask it to on purpose.

There are times when you get things. Be happy, attribute the receiving of it to your Guide, Highest Level Guide, the Guardian, your Angel, your Team, your Counsel—whatever name works for you. We do have the answers. We do have the best path for you. We do have the best ability to see what

Chapter 11 ~ Manifesting On Purpose

you are manifesting and why and to steer you toward more of it or away from it.

Your super-attractor within can do none of those things. It simply creates your life without your permission. Much of what it does, it does from the standpoint of automatic. Automatic retrieval. Automatic amplifying of what it has in its coffers.

What you think you know about the psyche of the mind is very small, but I like that you know some. You may want to argue because of the words on this page with me. If I were sitting there next to you, would you have a debate, would you want to debate? Or would you sit with a pen and notebook and take notes? Where is your emotional countenance in this moment?

I want you to be still. I want you to not argue. I want you to not debate when it comes to written word from those of us that are in the dimension where All That Is, is.

What is in the dimension of All That Is? It is the origination point of everything. Everything begins with an idea; everything is born from love. We are consciousness in our home environment. You are consciousness inside a body, inside an earth plane where things are unnatural or unreal or different. All of those words are equally true. Easier said, the way that you exercise what you are able to do in the physical world, in the physical body, is different than what you would do if you were not in the physical world or the body and resided here, back home.

In this dimension I are speaking from, things happen quickly. You identify what you want, you think upon it, you gather the energies or the people and their knowledge on it, and then you make it same or different, depending on what it is that you are doing. You are do-ers in the nonphysical. All of us. We do things. We have no day and night, but if we want to experience day and night, we just make it. We have no need to, but we could. If we did, we would perceive the experience in as much detail as we wanted.

The same goes for where you are. You create by your thoughts; however, there are many differences, the main one being you do not know that you are creating by your thoughts, and because you do not know it you have not gravitated toward the ability to identify your own thoughts and hold them close to you. If you could, you would hand-select the thoughts that you wanted to amplify. You would locate and spend time extrapolating detail, adding detail, and creating something. You might do it for fun. You might do it for purpose. The human mind does not have the ability built-in to hold your thoughts within your sphere of etheric.

Each of you walk around with an invisible bubble. It does exist. They can overlap. If you are sitting close to someone in the movie theater, they are overlapping. What does that mean? It means that you could walk away with their mood or their thought. Not so much their mannerisms, because those are built over time. Although if you are married or partnered up, siblings included, and you sit next to each other often—on the school bus every day, at dinner every day, at breakfast every day—and there is consistent repetition in what each of you are thinking about as you are sitting next to each other, you could co-create mannerisms based on the overlap.

It is an interesting phenomenon, but is it useful? No.

Chapter 11 ~ Manifesting On Purpose

I want you to ask for that co-creator-in-spirit, your High Guide, to tend to that ability, tend to your overlap. Tend to it. What does that mean? Simply this: if there is a good exchange, amplify it, make it useful. If it is already useful, make it more so. If it is not useful, create a barrier so that you do not become influenced from it.

Can we do that? Yes. Will we? Absolutely. There is nothing that we do not help you with. Why do you need to ask? Because the human mind receives vibrational tone from all directions. When you ask, it places emphasis on your desire for the inner-mind to place its preference on us. Over time, it will. It is a learning environment for the psyche of the mind that you are in.

The eternal validity of the Soul is intact. Lifetime after lifetime, after lifetime, after lifetime, you bring aspects of it more forward. The aspects are at the request of your Higher Self, that Divine Being that decided to have a life, and you are it. Those are the things that are built-in or easy. There is always a purpose behind which things are brought more forward. Your entire Being is inside of you. Is with you. Is aware of your life.

You are not aware of those other lives. Even when you meditate you are not aware of them. It is built-in for that to be the case. It is good that you are not carrying forward all of the personalities that you have ever been. You would be in mass confusion because every lifetime is different. Even a lifetime that is similar, a generation or a century apart, is too dissimilar for it to be useful. Add to that Birth Intentions, which adds another layer of dissimilarity.

The purpose or the reason for your life, the path of your

life, has a different weaving, has a different tale, and your Higher Self wants that one told. The aspects of you that are hidden from view have knowledge that is resident, experiences that are varied. Not all of those experiences are good for you, even though all experiences, from the perspective of All That Is, are valuable. They are not all valuable for the life that you are trying to live.

There are some that will understand that perfectly. There are others that will still be somewhat confused by it. So, I offer you this: do you want to re-experience your very worst day? I think not. Do you want to experience someone else's very worst today, and let's assume that their worst day is far worse than yours? I think not. Now multiply that by infinity. You have no reason to want to go backward, but some of you attempt to. What I want you to do is to look forward. If there is a need or a reason to bring another lifetime or aspects of a different lifetime, aspects of the Being that is the Greater Part of you, more forward, then that High Guide of yours will, automatically. You do not need to know about it nor ask for it.

If you are curious, have a reading from a qualified channel and we will tell you about it. Do not attempt to bring forward a lifetime that is not your own by yourself. Do not believe in what people tell you on this subject. People are curiosity-seekers. They are make-believe makers. I am not. I am an entity from within The Jeshua Collective and I am the Teacher of these things. Not only through this woman, Carol, but also through others before her. It is what I like to teach about the most.

Past-life regression is not good for you. You have the

Chapter 11 ~ Manifesting On Purpose

ability to open your minds up to retrieval and there your ability ends. What will you retrieve? Who will you retrieve and how much? You do not know. Someone who is certified in hypnotism, he/she does not know either. They can try to guide you. They can make suggestions that your mind might listen to. But the mind might not.

Back to the green carpet. Your mind might be okay with green carpet, even though every argument you ever had was standing on a green carpet. It might not take notice of what is directly in front of you. And so it goes with suggestion while under hypnosis. It might have an effect; it might not, because the interior mind may have its mind set on something. You do not know what, or whether that is the case.

If it finds what it is looking for, it is satisfied. It does not mean that the aspects of whatever lifetime it bumped into or found is going to aid you in whatever it is that you think you are after. It is exploratory examination of your Soul. That is not a good idea. Do not do it. If you ignore these words and do it anyway, then ask for your Highest Guide to step in and do what needs to be done for it to be useful. They are always guiding you, but when you, as I have said before, make a direct asking that involves your Guide or Guide Team, then you invoke a request that your inner-mind listens to.

Do not ask moments before you go under hypnosis. The mind needs to be prepared for such a journey. How long depends on who you are. A year in advance for some, yes! A month in advance for some, yes. A week in advance? Never. Not one of you. People say leave it up to the professionals, and when it comes to past-life regression through hypnosis,

I agree.

    The professionals, however, do not come in human form. They come in Guide form of the nonphysical kind.

    When we do it, we call it "activation of the psyche" of a lifetime. We not only select the lifetime, but the specific aspects and the timeframe when those aspects were in alignment with what you are needing help with. We are precise when we do it and we do not need your permission. If your life and its weavings have created your life's story in such a way that an aspect of a previous you are useful, we bring it in automatically. That, too, is built-in.

    It comes with the territory of being the High Guide. Every Being that has that role is exquisite at what they do. There is no error because we do not make mistakes. Anyone that is interested in ocularity needs to understand that more fully. We do not make mistakes. Your human mind has resistance. Your human mind carries doubt. Your human mind holds the key to your life path. If you carry fear and aggravation—unworthiness to any degree—you have resistance. You have human-made limitation.

    There is no limitation in the life that you are living, except for that which you have made. This life that you are living can catapult you not into oblivion, but into glory by way of your thoughts.

    What do you want to create? If wealth is your goal, narrow down your timing and your subject and keep your eyes on the prize. Stay off the subject of doubt and do not alter your components. Do not alter your components! "I want A, B, C and D, and I want it to come easy and I want to be satisfied the entire time." That is the perfect statement

Chapter 11 ~ Manifesting On Purpose

because you have added the two components that most of you forget: having it come easy and enjoying the journey. "I want these components. I want it to come easily and enjoy the entire journey."

Let that be the sentence you wake up to and the sentence you fall asleep to. Let your High Guide take care of the rest. Now, how do you accomplish a feat of any size if you do nothing? You cannot. There are things that you have to do to activate the becoming of having something. It might be a phone call, it might be knocking on doors, it might be buying something, it might be selling something, it might be getting off the couch. If you sit and meditate and doodle twenty-four-seven and do nothing, will you have that thing that you are wanting? You might. Will you have it in the timeframe you are wanting? You might not.

It depends whether or not during that doodling and meditation session, any good ideas came to you. If they did, get up and do them because it might prove useful for you. It might have been given to you to clear away some aggravation point inside the mind that is not useful. Sometimes the mind needs to be satisfied on something that it is focused on before it will allow your High Guide to bring evidence of what you are wanting to you, or bring the actual thing/situation for you to enjoy.

You might need to follow through on some things because you do not know what your mind is focused on. Yes, you can ask us and we can tell you in private consultations. That is what private guidance is for: to help you manifest a life you are happy with faster—and sometimes to simply manifest it at all.

Can we take poor focus of the inner-mind away? No, because your mind is your own. If it, the interior aspect of the mind that is focused on something, believes that you need to advertise your business, for example, you might need to. It is the driver of your life. You may say, "I do not need to spend money on advertising, I want this to come easy." But if advertising is a belief that your interior mind is holding onto, it might be something that needs to be satisfied. Therefore, it is your easiest path. We can tell you these things.

Maybe something good or useful or beneficial toward what you are asking for will come of the actions. Maybe not, but the most beneficial would be that the mind is satisfied. If it is, you are internally, and the mind can focus on the next steps for you. You might advertise and feel good about it, gain a customer or two or five hundred, and you might come upon a time where, without frustration, you decide that advertising is no longer necessary. The focus point has been satisfied and is no longer an obstacle.

You do not see the inner weavings of the psyche of the mind. Your Highest Guide does. It is that Being that is co-creating with you. When you want something, the Being in the nonphysical that is watching over you and your development as a human being and as a Spirit Being forms a Plan. That Guide tends to the Plan and yes, the Plan does change because you are not having side-by-side verbal conversations all the way through it.

We like when people ask what the Plan is and we will give it to you in small increments, enough for you to be satisfied to move forth and do. To have a good time. We will

Chapter 11 ~ Manifesting On Purpose

tell you when and how often to come back for more. Those of you that are very good students will have conversations with us on cue.

You have never manifested so easily, so quickly, so beautifully than with private one-on-one qualified, channeled conversations with us—The Jeshua Collective. I mention this now because we get to have influence on a human mind and we do not participate in that activity any longer. Your High Guide has this role, as we all had it before them.

Guidance will be concrete. "Do this and then this and then this for this long and then come back for more." Guided conversations are not necessary, but they sure are fun—for us and for you. It is fun to weave the energies together to send an intelligent thought angled through the dimensions all the way to the High Guide (or from them) to the human being, who transfers it to the inner-mind and then asks the inner-mind to say it through a channel to you. It is fun. It is also extremely useful for you.

It takes the frustration out. It is a two-way direct conversation that you are having with the ones that know you best in the spirit dimension. We want you to be comfortable getting those kinds of conversations. We want you to trust those kinds of conversations. We want you to come with questions. We want you to ask more questions. We want you to become qualified in delivering structured guidance as a channel yourself as well.

End chapter.

CHAPTER 12

The Number Sequence

*To masterfully manifest a life of abundance,
go from happy subject to happy subject
to happy subject to happy subject, preferably
all the way to just the tip of happy fading.
Then, back it up to happy ascending
and move on to another subject.*

Chapter 12 ~ The Number Sequence

Session: 15, video: #0697
November 16, 2021

When you figure out what you want, that is step one. We are going to run through the numbers. Numbers do not have a meaning, but you have decided that they do, so now they do and we use them. It is a useful analogy.

Number 1: You have an idea.

Number 2: You start amplifying the idea. It starts taking shape.

Number 3: When it takes shape to a certain degree, that High Guide of yours puts a Plan together.

Number 4: If you stick with it, you start to see a little glimmer of hopefulness in the idea and the having of it.

Number 5: It is drawing the attention of the super-attractor within and therefore it is on its way.

Number 6: This is the one that you do not want unless you are someone like Carol, and then you will say, "I want it, but I want it to be easy." That is exactly what we want all of you to say.

Number six is the stepping-stone to receiving. You either step forward or you do not. It is where most of you have that divergent path of going after something or dreaming about it. Wishful thinking or drive and determination. Number six is not drive. It is clearing the pathway, and if you are clearing the pathway that means that there are obstacles. How do you remove obstacles? You run over them. You run around them. You crawl underneath them. You plow through them. You pretend they are not there and smash up against them. They are there.

Guidance can help you maneuver around them, avoid the pitfalls or the landmines. What are the landmines? Blocks. Energy blocks. They are the things that have the most quantity. They are the skyscrapers versus the townhomes and the skyscrapers are blocking your path. How do you get over or around or under or through or beneath or avoid a skyscraper on the internal mind? You do not, and it is the reason why your thought patterns can be lockset on something that you do not want.

You can get the happy factor going and you can make good headway and you might start receiving some of it, but not the big stuff, not the juicy stuff. Not the really, really, really fun stuff. Not the abundance or opulence or whatever it is that you are wanting.

You get in a relationship, but you have some baggage. You get a business going and the bills are mounting but you like the idea. You have some both—I like it, I like it not. How do you get rid of whatever is holding you back? On your own, you do not. We see it. It is accumulation of thoughts that have created a barrier. It is a barrier within your etheric body.

Number six is determination to get through the barrier, and if you are happy you might shimmy through it unscathed and just feel some rough spots. If so, the barrier was not very thick. If the barrier is thick everything feels hard, seems insurmountable, or it just does not happen.

You want customers and they do not call you. That is a barrier. You have signage, you have a beautiful storefront, you have advertising, you have employees—and the people

Chapter 12 ~ The Number Sequence

do not walk through the door. Month after month after month, there is nothing until you decide to close up shop.

Do not get discouraged; get a reading from a qualified channel. If you find one and cannot pay for their services, then ask for a recommendation from them. Who will they recommend? A channel who charges less. But every channeler will always recommend another channel because they know beyond a shadow of a doubt that channeled readings are information from the High Guide—uncontaminated if the channel is full and open-tranced. Are we selling you on channeling yet? We hope so, because we want to talk to you directly without interference from the human being. We can identify the root of the problem (pun intended).

The Root part of the chakra system is where accumulation occurs. Accumulation is the metropolis. There are landscapes—not much happening; there are communities—there is something going on; and there is downtown with all the skyscrapers—the energy blocks. Are they enormous? Some. In all of you? Yes. That is why you cannot blink your eyes and have what you want right in front of you. It is not luck when you get something. It is positioning, alignment, and timing.

We do not call it luck. If it were, then anybody could do it. Not everybody can. The confluence of positioning, alignment, and timing might never occur for someone who has a block in one or more of them on a particular subject at a particular point in their life. It is a confluence of energies that you have created. Not the aspects of you from prior experiences, prior lifetimes. It is this lifetime. It is an accumulation of this lifetime's gunk.

What do you do about it? Positivity is powerful. It is more powerful than any other activity that you could put your mind on. Positivity on everything is good. Positivity on something that you are wanting is altogether the only thing that you ought to be doing. If something becomes uncomfortable, then go be happy on something else. Do not just distract yourself. Do not just move off the subject. Do not "just" do anything in this life. Go from happy subject to happy subject to happy subject to happy subject, preferably all the way to just the tip of happy fading. Then back it up to happy ascending and move on to another subject.

Sensitivity training is what this chapter will lead you to. Energy healing is what I am talking to you about now. Once you understand the confluence of thoughts, emotions, and accumulated energy, you will understand how to manifest anything. When you understand it fully, and you get the connection between who you are in the physical and who you are in the nonphysical, and who all of us are in the nonphysical and what this physical life can do and what it cannot do—then you have understood that we are Real.

When you understand that we are Real, then you will be able to go out and live your lives and manifest as much as you want in any area. You will be able to do whatever you want to do. But you will also have created an opportunity for the interior mind to have lengthier Teacher-student conversations with your High Guide.

When the mind is ready for that, your Unfoldment Plan (capitalize both) will be put together. The Unfoldment Plan is what your Divine Being—who you are in the nonphysical dimension—is wanting with your ocular abilities specifically.

Chapter 12 ~ The Number Sequence

"I would like to do this," your Higher Self says, "My person is on the path of learning how to communicate with us. I want them clean, clear, and accurate, and I want them to use it in this way. I want them to become this kind of person. It is useful in the development of our personalities."

Is it always the same for everyone? Yes and no. Why is that? Because every Higher Self wants you to have clear reception, unwaveringly accurate translation, and clean ability to produce the very thing that we conveyed in a way that you can understand it. Dissimilar, because no Being in the nonphysical Plans for you to use it as a professional reader, for example. Some simply want excellence with intuition to guide you to a very specific pathway on another topic. Varying degrees of using ocular abilities are acceptable. Do they ever not want you to be a channel? No. Do you stop short of completing the entire Unfoldment Plan? Most of you, yes. Does that matter? No. Do we have an Unfoldment Plan that you cannot become? No.

We know what you are wanting in life, that Divine Being in conjunction with your High Guide creates your Unfoldment Plan. Together, they know who you are, what you are desiring in your own life—you the physical person, what all your goals and vision boards are, what all your aspirations are, what your personality is like, what you at this moment in time are able to manifest.

Therein lies the basis of the Teacher-student relationship for your Unfoldment. That is why a human teacher straightforward is not who you ought to be receiving lessons from. Do go to them for your development circles, for your practice sessions. Just do not believe that the teacher is teaching you. They are a facilitator of organized practice. That is our Knowing on what should occur.

This interior mind, it is finicky. You do not know when it begins to believe that this teacher who is holding the session is the Teacher. If your internal psyche of the mind, your inner-mind, starts to believe that the human being is the Teacher, then it starts to resist the lessons that are coming to it vibrationally from your High Guide. The reason is simple, really. The inner-mind learns vibrationally, and a human being does not speak vibrational technology; you speak words, and words do not teach the inner-mind. You will learn slower. A lot slower.

We want development circles to occur and, if we had our preference, they would have no leader, but would have at least one channel present to validate for you and to answer any questions, as well as give you the exercises. We are watching what each of your minds are doing, how much each mind is paying attention, and what the best lesson is. Through a channel we get to teach you directly!

I transition this chapter now to the Beings who are the Unfoldment Team.

We are the Guide Team now. We have begun to teach the mind of you, dear reader. We are watching your inner-mind. We are watching your responses. We are watching your emotional responses. We are watching what your intellectual abilities are, but we are not concerned about them. We are moving energies around on the inside of your energy field so that your inner-mind receives more influence from the words in this book.

We are the ones that activate the interior mind to do what

Chapter 12 ~ The Number Sequence

needs to be done to help you learn to receive accurately. Accuracy is foremost on all of our minds because accuracy is necessary for you to receive in abundance in your lifetime.

Through the Unfoldment, your personal Plan is enacted. The Plan is not how much money you will make; it is what will be taught and in what order and to what degree.

Person A, Person B, and Person C, they are all approaching the opportunity for an Unfoldment Plan. Person A has verbal tendencies. Person B has visual tendencies. Person C has sensations only. Their Plans can be greatly varied, or they can be identical. The curriculum and the order of each topic will always be different because your interior minds are different. The Plans might be identical because the decision from your Higher Self could be the same.

How can you have a class of more than one if we are teaching each mind independently, much less twenty or thirty or fifty or hundred or thousand students at a time, or an online self-paced program and still follow the Unfoldment Plan, exactly? You cannot. But unless you have private instruction throughout your Unfoldment, you will be in groups. We do not advise self-taught, because your own interior mind will create error after error after error, and your accuracy will suffer for it permanently in this lifetime.

It is that important that you have a second person to help you. That second person can be anyone because you need validation. If you are living on your own and you sit down and you meditate and you have your logbook and you attempt to receive, write it down. Then ask who that information was for. Your High Guide will tell you. Or ask a question like this, "Tell me something about my mother."

Then you already know who the information is about and then go to your mother for validation. If your mother is not available or is deceased, then ask someone else who would know. You will validate, little by little, some or all of what you received this way.

It is important for you on both fronts to have some things validated as accurate, as well as understand that not everything can be validated. Some things will also be inaccurate altogether. But inaccurate could also be poor memory on the topic for the person that you asked on the day that you asked them. So, we say accurate or not fully accurate.

The Unfoldment Team are Beings who do this as a vocation. It is our chosen passion. We do many other things, but this is what we love to do. We step in when your High Guide has asked for us. You need not know that it is us. But it is good for your interior mind to know that there are many Beings in spirit who have banded together to guide you.

Throughout your life, we do (some of us) step in at certain times, certain phases, for certain reasons, and then we stay with you throughout the balance of your life. Once we are called upon, we do not leave you. Ever. When we step in, we step in and we are there for the duration.

I am resuming this chapter from the Unfoldment Team and thank them for their generous contribution. Their involvement was at my request. I could have explained what was explained myself, but I like allowing others to describe what they do on occasion. I also like how they described it.

There are those of us that teach for a living, so to speak, and there are those of us that do what has been taught for

Chapter 12 ~ The Number Sequence

a living. I enjoy teaching. I teach Unfoldment in this place where I am and this team of Unfoldment Beings are my students. They are learned Beings. I will always be their Teacher because that is who I am to their Being. I am their Master Teacher and they are Master Students. There is no higher than Master Student, unless that Being decides that they want to teach the subject. So they are simply exquisite, or Masters, or have reached mastery. Those that have spoken in this chapter have all reached mastery.

Was there more than one? Yes. How when there was only one voice? It is easy for us to do. We design the curriculum, we identify the words, and then we stream them through the dimensions, and place them in the hands of the High Guide who then delivers them to your mind. The High Guide then asks the mind to say them if that mind has been taught that skill, as Carol's has. That is a channel. If the High Guide was not there the information would go nowhere. That will never occur because there is always a High Guide; it is the way of it.

This team of Beings that we call The Guardian has one in that role. Every person has a team of Beings and one of those Beings is always identified as the High Guide role. There is another layer of Guides and another layer beyond that. Those are your Teachers and their Teachers. Your High Guide knows who and which and when to call upon them when you are ready for more. Your High Guide is a Being who knows exactly what to do, exactly when to call upon another, and exactly what you are needing. Always.

They are your Guardian. Your Highest Guide steps in when asked for a purpose or purposes which are dependent upon your life and what you are manifesting currently.

It is never required to get you back on your path. Your High Guide does not need help with that job. The additional levels of Teachers step in when you are ready for more only. It is the way of it. It will not change. And no, you cannot trade a High Guide in if your life is going downhill. They are perfect, and perfectly suited for the role that they are doing.

You, beautiful human being that you are, are needing to retune yourself to happy and re-educate yourself to what it means to be in alignment with your Guide. To affirm for yourself what it is that you are wanting and to recalibrate who you are. If those things are done, your life will turn around.

Be careful what you take in. Be careful what you listen to. Be careful to not overdo or oversell or overthink anything that feels upsetting. Do not over-believe human teachers. Do not overthink situations. Do not overemphasize the negative. The power of positivity is incredibly important, not only in your ocular development, but for you, for your life, for the world at large.

Mass consciousness does not evolve in a silo or a test tube on its own. It evolves one thought at a time. Every thought contributes to the whole. Every thought is important and every opportunity that you have to choose the happy or happier thought is recommended for anyone, any lifetime, during any age or era.

End chapter.

Chapter 12 ~ The Number Sequence

For those of you who noticed that the number sequence ended at six but is aware of the Teachings of Jeshua on them, here are the remaining three.

Number 7: Evidence of what you are wanting is found in abundance, but it is not yet yours. You are observing others, perhaps, or seeing images of it. Whatever it is that you are wanting is coming to you. Take this evidence as that only and do not discourage yourselves with doubt at the cause for it not being yours. Delight in it instead, for it is in the becoming.

Number 8: The object of your attention is yours in abundance.

Number 9: Your original idea or desire is complete, and you shift your gaze to something different, or the idea takes on a newness that is much bigger or incorporates elements that are substantially different.

CHAPTER 13

Your Identity

*The aspects of you that were hand-selected
form the basis of your personality
not your persona.*

Chapter 13 ~ Your Identity

Session: 16, video: #0698
November 16, 2021

Although most of you do not know who your Guide is, they know you. They have been with you your entire life. Truly, they have been with you since before this physical life began. I do want you to understand what a Spirit Guide is.

Spiritual communities have a good understanding that you have a Being in the nonphysical that watches over you and protects you. That you have Teacher Guides, Healer Guides, your "for a specific reason" Helpers.

People find many ways to describe what they know. Some things they know are good, some things are not. Who we are and what we are and why we do what we do is altogether misunderstood.

You are not beings who have forgotten who you really are. You have not forgotten. You have, however, evolved into a type of human being that does not rely on the pure tone of Source. Because of that, you have a Guardian. A Guardian is a collective of Beings that form together, remain together for your entire physical lifetime.

They are powerful. They are learned. They are experts in what they do. If they were not, they would not be doing that role. They do it when you are awake. They do it when you are asleep. What do they do? Everything that you are needing to remain in the physical dimension.

This is a perceived experience that you are having. Because of that, your Higher Self is doing something different than the Beings that have formed together as The Guardian. Blind Man's bluff: one person is pretending to be the seeker and everyone else is running around. Different scenario, but enough of an analogy that you can understand.

Your Higher Self is remaining thoughtful in a way that allows you to have a physical life. You were created before this life experience. The Soul of you was determined and focused you into being. All of you begin life prior to entering the physical form that you are in. There was a beginning before your beginning, and that beginning is the beginning.

It was identified by that Higher Power of you to have another incarnation, and that incarnation would include certain aspects of the multitude of lifetimes that came before you. Everything does not come forward. Certain things do, and they are on purpose and for a purpose. If every aspect of every life came forward, you would have no true identity. You would be an accumulation of all, and you would be confused. It would also be highly unimaginative. Not useless, but would not allow you to grow and learn, to home in on one or more qualities that you wanted, to do something more or different.

The underlying aspects of you that were brought forward were hand-selected to be the foundation of your identity. That is who you are at the core of you. You are not identical to anyone, because even those aspects of you have nuances that are your own based on experiences that your multitude of lifetimes—substitute personalities—have accumulated.

Some of you now understand built-in. Athleticism can be built-in; height, not. Generous can be; laughter, not. Determination can be; to become a rock star, not. There is an endless supply of ideas. The aspects of you that were hand-selected form the basis of your personality, not your persona.

Chapter 13 ~ Your Identity

They are the interior you. The exterior you, however, is born of the world based on influence and what your inner-mind has decided, as, "I like it, I like it not."

Physical attributes (bone structure, color of your hair)—there are some genetics involved because you have evolved into people that have segregated themselves in that way. We call that lineage. In the physical, your lineage.

We call your accumulation of lifetimes "ancestry." Get used to it because we will not change those terms. Lineage, within the world. Ancestry, prior to the world—prior to the world only because you are in both places. You are not there and then in the world and then go back home. That is altogether misunderstood, and we correct your learning on it. The inner-mind is listening to the words of this book and we will not teach it false lies to confuse it further.

You are having a physical life experience. You are not YOLO ("you only live once"). You are not. You began this life prior to entering the physical world and becoming the human being that you are.

You are also duality of existence. That Higher Self of you remains non-physically focused and will, forever more. It is not possible to have a physical life experience separated from the dimension where All That Is, is.

The life experience that you are having is being understood and taken in, recognized by, appreciated by that Higher Self of you as you are living it—not after you pass from this world. They know who you are. They know what you are. They know why you are what you are. You do not. They see the weavings. They see the patterns. They see the accumulation of energies that have caused you to be who you are today. They judge you not. They reprimand you not.

They do love you. They do love that you are having a physical life experience. They do know that you are not aware of the patterns that energy creates within your etheric field. Energy work is something that the world is starting to believe in. You do not understand what it is, but it is energy without fail. Energy is who you are. It is how you create. It is how you miscreate and it is how you change what you are creating. Playfully, now we say manifest and de-manifest your life.

We want you to do it on purpose. We want you to have positive thoughts. We want you to have positive memories. We want you to have positive interaction. We want it to be full of vigor and fun and eagerness and joy, and laughter (lovemaking included, as long as it is pleasurable, physically, mentally, emotionally, thoughtfully).

Ailments of the body, we agree, are caused from what you now call stress. Substitute stress for coagulation of dense thought patterns that have knotted together and caused a stoppage in the free flow of energy. Put a cork in a bottle, water does not come out. Stoppage.

It is not desired for energy to not flow. It needs to flow to be healthy. Circulation is necessary. If your circulatory system had a stoppage, you would have a problem of varying degrees. Your etheric body, though dissimilar, is also similar in that stoppages create unwellness.

It starts in the etheric and moves to the physical or the mental. Mental can then be moved into thought patterns, behavioral patterns, emotional patterns. Physical moves into the cellular structure of something. We teach you how to

Chapter 13 ~ Your Identity

unclog the stoppages of energy. Your stress levels internally decrease, and if they decrease significantly or significantly enough, then you experience change for the better. You slow down, you argue less, you are clear-minded, you are more thoughtful, kinder, more forgiving, more patient. You have more charisma, more confidence or self-esteem. Then your life changes for the better.

Energy work is necessary. There are ways for you as an individual to do it on yourself. There are ways for you to do it on others. It is maintenance that people can do on people, animals, plants—anything that has biological components. There are touch points that can be activated. When those touch points are activated in the right sequence for the right amount of time, by the proper touchpoint (activator), then circulation in the proper direction speeds up.

It is like a fan. You turn it on, air blows in one direction. Things that were lying still or slowly moving are now blown in the direction of the airflow created by the fan. It is very similar. Energy is moved in the right direction, and it picks up where it left off every time you do it.

You can heal your bodies over time. You can do preventative maintenance as well as corrective. However, corrective does take longer because you have to de-manifest first. It means there are more things that need to be done, more healing needs to take place.

There is also Source Healing. There are many fancy terms for it. The new one that Carol has come across, which is accurate, sounds awkward to her, but she also likes the term—quantumness. Quantum Healing. It is healing at the micro, micro, micro cellular level. It is healing at the level

Mind Body Connection

that is right, because the energies are identified by your High Guide and directed to the specific point in your body that requires it. Then the energies are moved.

For that work you must be able to focus on nothing and remain in a trance state for a long enough period of time that we can flow healing tones through the dimensions and angle them towards the thing that is requiring healing. If you are a human being who can easily move into an altered state and you can hold that altered state and feel the physical sensation that goes along with it and remain there with little to no thought—then we can heal through you.

We do not do superficial healing. We heal that which is of the world. We prefer to heal through a channel who remains in a trance state that has the ability to verbalize for us or has allowed us to teach the mind how to let us select the words and phrases and ask the mind to say them. They are identical. Some people will prefer one definition over the other, so we offer both of them to you.

A trance channel can remain in an altered or trance state and talk. We do the talking and we do the healing. That way, the human being (presumably) who is receiving the healing gets educated on what is being done and entertained by some of the things that the channel can see or feel or hear to validate the connection. The human being that was receiving the healing has something to think back on to value and remember and believe in the healing session.

End chapter.

CHAPTER 14

Aura-Seekers

*Meditation, which includes breath work
and energy work routinely,
is essential to remaining happy.
It is essential for receiving what we call
the Glad Effect, to being able to manifest,
and for receiving verbal communication
from your Guide.*

Chapter 14 ~ Aura-Seekers

Session: 17, video: #0700
November 16, 2021

The etheric field is unseen by the untrained eye, and by that I mean everyone. There are some people (we call them aura-seekers) who can see the shimmer that is the uppermost layer of the outer band of energy. It comes across generally as a color or a line of color. It is not, however, the energy field. It is—listen carefully now—the outermost layer of the energy field because it is closest to you, the aura-seeker.

If a rust color or darker is seen, there is anger in the human being. There might also be anger in the seeker, for dark is what they picked up on. If blue or golden is seen, then the person is feeling peaceful or is humble by nature. "The person," meaning who is being seen or "the seeker," since the mood of the seeker can alter what they see. It is an interesting ability.

If you have or learn this ability, I want you to use it for good, to identify vibrations emanating from a person and use them. I want you to begin with yourself. If you see those deeper tones in someone's aura, move away. It is not time to engage with that person. Even if you are happy in that moment, your happiness is not enough to alter their mood. If it is your mood affecting what you see, then you are not a good candidate for their engagement.

Aura-seeking is a useful ability. But if you believe that you can fix another and use this colorful external sight ability and dream up ways of bringing people to you so that you can give them your happy disposition, you are not helping yourself. You are drawing more dense energies to you. In every case, every person, every time.

If you teach yourself, and you can, to be an aura-seeker, heed these words—always use it to identify who or what to engage with. Blue and golden are your first choices. Orange and pink, second choice. Greenish, third choice. Darker tones, last.

If you have no option to walk away and not engage from a darker-tone-emitting person, let your engagement be swift and to the point. Do not make demands of your own emotional state. It is not necessary for you to fix another human being. They have their own suite of Guides that are already tending to that individual's mood or outlook.

Always use this ability as an indicator, advance notice, and do not try to do what your human emotional countenance is not equipped to do. You cannot change dense tones within the psyche of the human mind. If you see it, it is resident through the layers into the innermost layer of the human, and it needs no help from human beings.

It does not mean that the human being is a lost cause. It means that they have a flare-up internally and you might experience their anger. It does not mean that you cannot pay attention to them at a different time, because a different day they may be a different color. A different moment, they might be a different color. When you stop thinking about whatever you are thinking about, your colorful expressions that are found in the etheric change. It is simply advance notice.

The etheric field itself is completely invisible to the human eye. You cannot train yourself to see this energy bubble around you. We have described it over the ages in many different ways as swirls, as lines, as bands, as hula-

Chapter 14 ~ Aura-Seekers

hoop-like, as layers, as mist that overlaps. All are good descriptions.

They are *not* horizontal. Some are vertical. Some are twisting. Some are looping. Some are shifting. There is an outer layer of the etheric so that it becomes a closed-loop system. It is what we refer to as the chakras, the energy points, the vortexual openings, the communication pipeline, and the pipeline of life. The energy field itself is the chakratic system.

It is, for almost all of you, wide enough to overlap with people that you are sitting or standing or lying near. If you are thinking of someone, you are also overlapping the Crown. It is telepathic communication that occurs when you overlap the Crown. If you are in a bad mood, step away and do not think about that person. There are many things that can happen when the energy fields overlap. There is no time-space-reality. You do connect with people regardless of geographic distance because the Crown is available to all.

It is communication at large, and within it is your connection to the nonphysical dimension. The Source of Life that created you and the suite of Beings that we call The Guardian surround your Crown. It is masterful how it is all put together.

We give you these descriptions so that you have our Knowing on who you are. You are a physical person. You are a nonphysical Being.

Your physical person includes things that are visible and invisible. Your nonphysical Being is aware of you, is Alive, is Real, is having your life experience with you and is who you will shift with during your Transition.

Mind Body Connection

The energy field itself was not meant to be cloudy. You cannot see the cloudiness. We can. We can see where energy is beginning to coagulate and, depending on where it is, we are able to tell you what you are currently manifesting physically, emotionally, mentally, in your relationships, in your financial wellness, in your interaction with others, and in your behavioral patterns.

It is good to remove cloudiness from your lives. When you do, you become clear-sighted. It is a good description. The bright, clear mind, or a hazy, overcast way of thinking. We want you to strive not for anything in this world. Doing meditation, which includes breath work and energy work routinely, is essential to remaining happy. It is essential for receiving what we call the Glad Effect, to being able to manifest, and for receiving verbal communication from your Guide, Loved Ones, Angelic Ones, and those that are hovering about, guiding you, that we call Helpers.

For the mind to be aware of us, the opportunity is yours. We are wanting you to not only have an interest in it, but to lean into it so far that you plunge into and swim about in this thing we call Source-Led living.

It is delicious. It is delightful. It is altogether the best life experience that you could have. Clarity comes when you can receive clean, clear, and accurate verbal guidance.

It was a joy to have had this conversation with you. I am hoping to have many like it with you in the future.

End chapter and book. We are complete.

Opportunities to Engage with Jeshua

Private Consultations with Jeshua:

Workshops are a great way to receive guidance from Source but sometimes there's nothing like a one-on-one, private conversation for readings and energy work. Jeshua is the collective of nonphysical Teachers that are gentle, wise, and straightforward yet compassionate. With pin-pointed accuracy, they know what you need to know and how to bring clarity to your life. Remove fear and doubt on your ability to manifest love, happiness, and all things in abundance.

Workshops with Jeshua:

The Powerfulness of Source Energy –
The Four Pillars of Learning

This workshop has been designed as a two-day weekend and five-day cruise workshop series, with both options giving you over fourteen hours of engagement with Jeshua. Each workshop begins with The Foundational Material and how knowing who your Guide is helps your intuitiveness. Day one wraps up with law of attraction and an in-depth study on manipulation of thought using creative wordplay. Day two begins with stretching exercises and why they aid self-healing, followed by an array of touch-point activation methods that anyone can do. The workshop ends with a segment on Intuitive Development and validation on the how, why, and when to reach for guidance. A portion of each segment includes Q&A to ensure you have all the tips, tools, and takeaways to help you live your life On Purpose.

Our Knowing – Conversations with Jeshua

The most powerful teachings on law of attraction and connection with your Guide team available! Jeshua expands the conversation of law of attraction and the power of positivity by combining it with teachings on natural healing to clear away the unconscious beliefs that are holding you back from intentional manifesting. Energy work plus positivity equals you "getting stuff." These completely channeled events are your opportunity to engage directly with Jeshua, with your questions guiding the conversation. Their teachings leave you with concrete understanding and actionable steps that are easy to implement.

Classes with Jeshua (partial list, see website for current schedule):

Unfoldment Into Channeling –
Your Gateway to Intuitive Development

Jeshua Is. They are Consciousness. They are Infinite Intelligence. They are Source Beings. Their guidance always produces results because they are the Teachers—they explain why. They know how our minds work, where you are in your development, what your skills are, and what your Guide wants you to know about your progress. They increase your confidence—as well as your accuracy. There is no better way to learn how to communicate with your Guide and Loved Ones than with channeled instruction. Antioch from the Jeshua Collective leads discussion topics to combine exploratory and cognitive-based learning to aid your development. They not only teach you exercises and validate your progress but also who "nonphysical Beings" are and why guidance from them is so important.

Opportunities to Engage with Jeshua

The Art of Self-Healing

Directing Energy to Self-Heal is the focus of this class. Elohim from the Jeshua Collective has created a program designed for healthy living, no matter who you are, how old you are, and what your current health status is. This life is meant to be lived happy, healthy, and prosperous. Directing Source Frequency through your etheric "grid" clears your mind and body of unconscious beliefs by a little or a lot, depending on your commitment to it. There are ways to heal and there are ways to create healing—Jeshua shows you both.

A Course In Miracles Explained

Reality is the one you create for yourself. Words matter. Thoughts matter. Choosing the better thought, the better idea, the better situation, the better feeling, is the miracle. Through me, Jeshua gives insight to the teaching behind and how to implement A Course In Miracles in your own life. Students are encouraged to join the public Facebook group Spiritually Led Journey as a means to help create more loving kindness in social media.

I AM Intensive

A chakra-cleansing, three-day retreat-style workshop, the "I AM" was designed by Jeshua to heal your Root Chakra from unwanted habits, unconscious beliefs, and painful memories that stop you from manifesting the life you are wanting AND the life purpose(s) your Higher Self Intended for you. A clear connection with your Guide is always one of the intentions for the weekend's activities, and increased connection is often the result. It is a belief-altering, life-changing, habit-reforming, Source-connected, inspiration-filled weekend that you will not soon forget. It is your restart button.

About the Author

Carol Collins, named Top 10 Women to watch by LA Weekly, is the original channel for The Jeshua Collective. Much to her surprise, her abilities spontaneously manifested in March 2019. After nine months of quiet meditation, "face-spelling" was introduced as a means of direct communication, followed by "voice-giving" (trance channeling) within a few weeks. Through her, Jeshua teaches about the Four Pillars of learning—collective consciousness, manifesting with ease, health and wellness through natural healing, and intuitive studies bringing out the natural abilities of communicating with Source in everyone—which They call The Essential Material. Carol offers private sessions with Jeshua for readings and attunements daily; retreats, and signature workshops frequently. She has been interviewed by celebrity personalities, featured in over two dozen magazines, has an extensive list of courses available in the Jeshua's Center for Intuitive Studies. In her third year of channeling Jeshua wrote eleven books through her—with more on the way. The first, Ocularity of the Mind, was released in fall 2022 and reached #1 for New Releases on its Amazon debut.

You're invited to contact and follow Carol:

Website: www.thepittsburghmedium.com
Email: carol@thepittsburghmedium.com
Facebook: The Pittsburgh Medium and The Teachings of Jeshua Fan Page
Instagram: The Pittsburgh Medium
Peloton ID: EatLoveBike
YouTube: The Pittsburgh Medium

www.ingramcontent.com/pod-product-compliance
Lightning Source LLC
Chambersburg PA
CBHW071416160426
43195CB00013B/1712